BIBLE BLOSSOM
STORYTELLER'S HANDBOOK

BIBLE BLOSSOM

STORYTELLER'S HANDBOOK
The Unfolding Story of God

written by
REV. RYAN CARTER AND REV. DR. DON L. DAVIS

with illustrations by
TIM LADWIG

TUMI Press • 3701 East 13th Street North • Wichita, Kansas 67208

Table of Contents

THE STORY OF GOD IN CHRIST: THE FULLNESS OF TIME

Lent: The Lowliness of Christ

Holy Week: The Passion of Christ

Eastertide: The Resurrection of Christ

Eastertide: The Ascension of Christ

Pentecost: The Coming of the Holy Spirit

Kingdomtide: The Last Times – The Story Continues Today

Acknowledgments and Dedication

A work as sophisticated and complex as *Bible Blossom: The Unfolding Story of God* demanded input from numerous people and contributors. Tim Ladwig served as our graphic illustrator, whose amazing drawings and illustrations provide primary shape to our telling of the story in this resource. Carolyn Hennings, our curriculum designer, put together the text, pictures, and graphics of the resource. Her eye for beauty and design are the source of the guide's structure, and its rich and clear presentation. Rev. Ryan Carter's refreshing theological and biblical expertise outlined much of the content in both the *Storybook* and the *Storyteller's Handbook*. Lorna Rasmussen, our Chief Project Officer, kept us all on track, on budget, and happily persistent in this multi-year effort.

We joyfully dedicate this resource to Rev. Terry Cornett, former head of Mission Studies with World Impact, and Dean Emeritus of The Urban Ministry Institute. Terry and Julie served faithfully as World Impact missionaries for twenty-five years, ten years of which he served as Academic Dean and Julie as the TUMI Librarian. From the summer of 2010, he and I began serious discussions on both the necessity and structure of such a resource – countless hours of debate and reflection produced clear and convincing

Early stages of Bible Blossom development

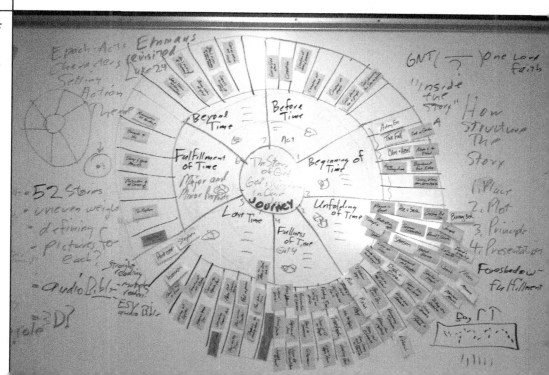

outlines of how we should design both the *Storybook* and the *Storyteller's Handbook*. Terry's theological clarity, spiritual depth, and brilliant teaching and missions experience is woven throughout these resources. As a gifted teller of the Tale of tales, it is only appropriate to acknowledge his contribution to this remarkable tool for theology, worship, spiritual formation, and witness.

Our sincere prayer is that the Chief Storyteller of God's story, the Holy Spirit, will use this resource to draw people of all ages and backgrounds to the story's hero and chief protagonist, the Lord Jesus Christ. We at the Institute love the story of God, and shape our entire lives around it. Jesus of Nazareth is the one for whom the story is being told, and who will fulfill its true meaning in his return for his people. May all who use this guide learn to tell this amazing story well, helping those who hear its episodes come to know him who himself joined the story to ensure our salvation and hope.

Rev. Dr. Don L. Davis
Wichita, Kansas
June 14, 2019

Telling Tales:
A Bible Blossom Primer on Storytelling

Introduction

At TUMI, we have dedicated ourselves in all our curriculum and training to raise up a generation of storytellers and story-indwellers who can preach, teach, sing, and embody the Story with power before their family members, neighbors, associates, and strangers.

Our entire enterprise in Sacred Roots is to help urban dwellers learn and be transformed by the simple Story of God's love, the tale of a caring, sovereign Lord who became one of us, who took on our nature and entered our human history to redeem creation and a people for himself. This striking, awesome, and true Story can bring revival to our weak and struggling churches. If we hold on to the Story as it is told in the Bible, summarized in the Creeds, and embodied in the Great Tradition we will multiply disciples. You see, the Story is true, powerful, and it is ours. No communion or tradition owns it; it belongs to the entire Church, and will transform all who are willing to give themselves over to its wonder and glory.

In the Kingdom Story, as in all great stories, you simply can never know who it is you have encountered, or what is truly happening. Things are more than what they appear to be. Dead messiahs rise again, and meek disciples wind up inheriting the earth. Can you see it?

In God's Story, the weak shame the strong, and the poor are rich in faith and heirs of the Kingdom. In God's Story, the first will be last and the last first. In God's Story, to be great in the Kingdom is to be the servant of all. Everything is topsy-turvy, upside-down, inside-out. To succeed in the Kingdom, you've got to be prepared to see things in a new way, to let the Story change the way in which you see and understand everything.

Why Story Matters

Story is the crux of God's revelation.

The Exodus Story

1. First, God acts in history to save his people.
    *   The Lord calls Moses to the enslaved Israelites (Exod. 3).
    *   He sends plagues against Egypt and Pharaoh (Exod. 4–11).
    *   His people slaughter a lamb at the first Passover, when all the firstborn of Egypt die (Exod. 12–13).
    *   Israel goes out of Egypt (Exod. 13).
    *   The Lord splits the Red Sea and they cross on dry land (Exod. 14).
    *   The Lord destroys their enemies when they try to pursue (Exod. 14–15).

2. As he does these things, he commands the Israelites to retell and reenact these events for future generations (Exod. 12.14–26, 26–27, 13.3–16).

3. Through the Law, the Lord gives the Jewish year as a cycle of retelling and reenacting the Exodus story (as well as coordinating with the harvest cycle). *[See facing page.]*
    *   Passover and Feast of Unleavened Bread – The Exodus
    *   Feast of Weeks – The Giving of the Law at Sinai
    *   Feast of Tabernacles – The Wilderness Journey

4. The story of the Exodus is the crux of revealing himself and forming for himself a people. *[See facing page.]*

5. Ultimately, 'God's Mighty Saving Acts' amount to his work in Jesus of Nazareth. The story of Christ and his kingdom, the Gospel, is the crux of all God's revelation.

6. Based on the Jewish year, Christians developed the Church Year as a cycle of retelling and reenacting the Gospel story.

Circle of Jewish Calendar

Robert Webber, *The Biblical Foundations of Christian Worship.* Peabody: Hendrickson, 1993. p. 191.

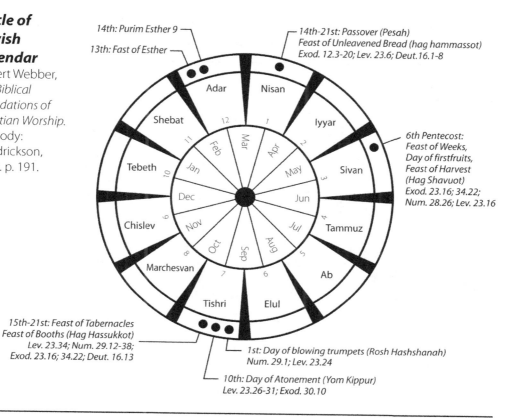

14th: Purim Esther 9

13th: Fast of Esther

14th-21st: Passover (Pesah)
Feast of Unleavened Bread (hag hammassot)
Exod. 12.3-20; Lev. 23.6; Deut.16.1-8

6th Pentecost:
Feast of Weeks,
Day of firstfruits,
Feast of Harvest
(Hag Shavuot)
Exod. 23.16; 34.22;
Num. 28.26; Lev. 23.16

15th-21st: Feast of Tabernacles
Feast of Booths (Hag Hassukkot)
Lev. 23.34; Num. 29.12-38;
Exod. 23.16; 34.22; Deut. 16.13

1st: Day of blowing trumpets (Rosh Hashshanah)
Num. 29.1; Lev. 23.24

10th: Day of Atonement (Yom Kippur)
Lev. 23.26-31; Exod. 30.10

Story: The Crux of Revelation

Rev. Ryan Carter

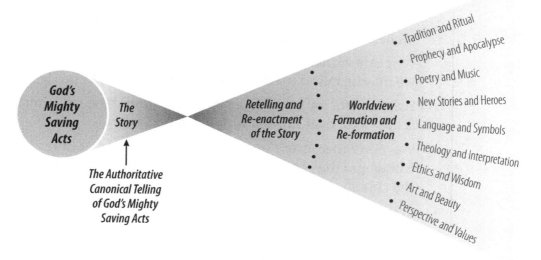

7. In broad outline we follow the life and ministry of Jesus and tread in his footsteps year after year.

The Plot Line of the Church Year
Rev. Ryan Carter

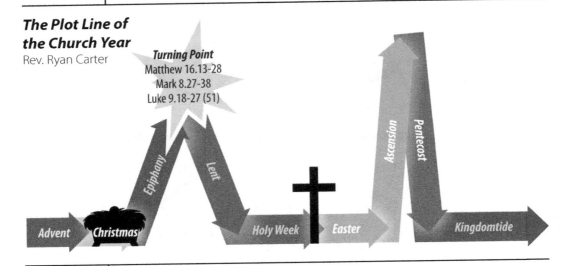

- We remember the promise and hope of Messiah through the long ages past (Advent).
- We celebrate the arrival of Messiah, born of a Virgin, laid in a manger in Bethlehem (Christmas).
- We walk with Jesus of Nazareth as he teaches and shows the world that the Kingdom of God is at hand (Epiphany).
- We follow Jesus, God's suffering servant, who humbly gives his life as a ransom for many (Lent).
- We share in the sufferings and death of Christ in order that we may be raised to new life in him (Holy Week).
- We shout for joy because Jesus is risen from the dead; Christ is the victor over sin, death, and Satan! (Easter).
- We remember Jesus's ascension to the right hand of the Father and the sending of the Holy Spirit to fill and empower the church (Ascension and Pentecost).
- In these last days the Spirit-filled church submits to the headship of Christ our Lord, labors for the harvest of Christ our Savior, and prepares the way for the second coming of Christ our King (Kingdomtide).

8. Year after year, the church patterns our life together on the story of Jesus in hopes that together we will be conformed to his image. The cycle of telling and picturing these stories broadens and enrichens the church with each year.

Following the Life of Christ throughout Each Year
Rev. Dr. Don L. Davis

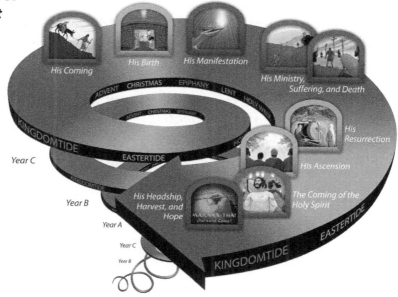

9. ICED: An acrostic for understanding how stories form and reform worldview

   • **I**dentity: our stories provide for us an understanding of ourselves and our personal worlds

   • **C**osmology: our stories enable us to make sense of our lives, and our place in the universe, it answers the big questions (i.e., where did we come from, why are we here, where are we going, what is most important, etc.)

   • **E**valuation grid: our stories become the plumbline by which we measure the truthfulness, rightness, and goodness of other competing visions and stories

   • **D**estiny: our stories give us a sense of the overall purpose of life, and speak to the big questions which human beings have asked and answered from the beginning (e.g., where do I go when I die, what is the ultimate purpose for living, what are my deepest concerns, how do I solve the critical issues of my life, etc.)

How to Understand Stories

All stories have a particular shape and possess a number of elements that make it possible to experience the truth of the story, whether historical or imaginative, in a way that is powerful, challenging, and entertaining.

The Compass of Narrative Elements: Charting a Course toward a Story's Meaning

Rev. Dr. Don L. Davis

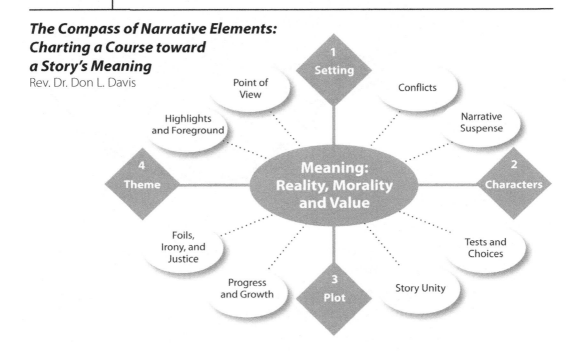

The Four Major Compass Points

1. The *setting* of the story
   - Place: where geographically is the story taking place?
   - Physical surroundings: what are the details physically?

- Temporal (time) setting: what are the time elements of the story?
- Cultural-historical surroundings: what details of culture or history are present?

2. The *characters* of the story
    - Who are the prime characters in the story? The "hero" and "villain"?
    - Note the precise order and details of the actions, conversation, and events of the characters.
    - How are the characters shown to us?
        - Direct descriptions
        - Indirect characterization
        - Appearance
        - Words and conversation
        - Thoughts and attitudes
        - Influence and effects
        - Actions and character
    - How are the characters tested, and what choices do they make?
    - How do the characters grow or decline (rise or fall) in the story?

3. The *plot* of the story
    - Note the exact order and details of the events and actions.
    - Note also how the story begins, develops, and ends.
    - Ask and answer questions about the actual plot.
    - Why did the events happen as they did?
    - Why did the characters respond as they did?
    - Could they have done things in a different manner?

- Five elements of plot
  - Introduction – How the story begins
  - Rising Action – Complications, conflicts, problems, issues, threats
  - Climax – Peak and turning point of the action
  - Falling Action – (Denouement) How the story resolves itself
  - Resolution – How the story ends

4. The *theme* of the story
   - What key principles and truths can be drawn out of this story?
   - What is the commentary on living portrayed in this story?
     - What is the story's view of reality (what is the world like, and what is our role in it?)
     - What is the story's view of morality (what constitutes good and bad in the story?)
     - What is the story's view of value and meaning (what is of ultimate concern and importance in the story?)
   - How do the truths of the story intersect with the challenges, opportunities, threats, and issues of our lives?

The Eight Smaller Compass Points

1. What plot conflicts exist within the story?
   - What are the central conflicts with God?
   - What are the central conflicts with others?
   - What are the central conflicts within the characters themselves?
   - What are the central conflicts between the character and their situation?

2. What are the aspects of narrative suspense revealed in the story?

   - What influences make us sympathize with the characters?
   - What produces disgust and aversion between us and the characters?
   - How are we made to approve of what the characters did?
   - What events or happenings cause us to disapprove of the characters?

3. How are the characters tested, and what choices do they make?

   - What is the dilemma/problem/conflict the protagonist is seeking to overcome?
   - What character quality is tested in the protagonist?
   - What alternative life choices are open to the characters in the story?
   - Which decisions do the characters make, and what is the result of their decisions?

4. How does the story unify itself in its various parts?

   - How does the organization of the story contribute to its unity?
   - What is the sequence of events in this story? (Beginning, Middle, and End)
   - In what way does the story's end resolve the questions raised at the beginning?

5. How do the characters progress and grow (or decline and fall) in the story?

   - Where do the characters begin in the story?
   - How do the experiences of the character affect their development?
   - Where do the individual characters eventually wind up as a result of their experiences, and the choices they made within them?

6. What foils, dramatic irony, and poetic justice are used in the story?

   • Foils: what characters are set against each other as foes in the story?

   • Dramatic irony: When is the reader informed of situations and realities that the characters themselves are unaware of?

7. What items are repeated, highlighted, and foregrounded in the story?

   • Repetition: what phrases, items, themes, issues, or actions are repeated?

   • Highlighting: what things in the characters and events are emphasized above other things?

   • Foregrounding: what things are made to stand out "center stage" in the flow of the story?

8. What is the author's point-of-view?

   • Note the author's comments about the characters and events.

     – Attitude (positive, negative, or neutral)

     – Judgment (negative or affirmative)

     – Conclusion (summarizing, absent, closure?)

   • Consider what voice the story is being written in:

     – The Omniscient narrator (the Holy Spirit)

     – The First-person testimonial

     – The Third-person narrator

The Art and Skills of Storytelling

Jesus's tale of the good Samaritan (Luke 10.25–37) is one of the most enduring stories ever told and illustrates well the art and skills of storytelling.

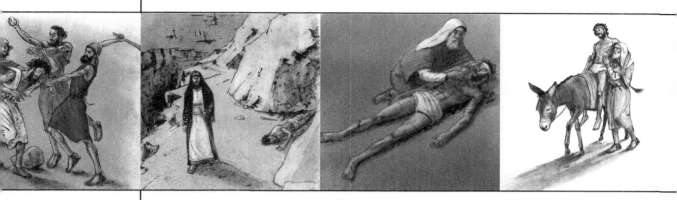

The I's of Storytelling the Word of God

Invite your audience to enter with you into the world of the story.

- In telling biblical stories we must find a way to invite our audiences into the story world as guests while we help them to take a tour of another world and another time.

- As tour leaders, we must get the attention of those who are now to become the guests of the world we are about to enter.

- Introduce a pertinent issue that is related to the story (Luke 10.25-30).

  - A theme under discussion (Luke 10.25)

  - A relevant question of interest or intrigue (Luke 10.26, 29)

  - A conflict or difficult issue (Luke 10.25–29)

  - Draw from the listener's experience, a slice of life to attend (Luke 10.30).

Illustrate the storyline and details of the story (Luke 10.31–35).

- Master the story yourself through multiple readings and long meditation.
  - Master the setting of the story.
  - Get to know the characters of the story.
  - Master the plot (storyline and timeline).
  - Discover the story's theme.

- Tell the story many times informally before you tell it formally in a teaching, counseling, or preaching setting: walk through the event before you provide a tour of it.

- Master the elements of oral language as a primary medium of storytelling.
  - Brief descriptions, short compact sentences
  - Picturesque, vivid language
  - Use of common, everyday language
  - Abundant use of strong verbs, active mode (not passive unless deliberate)
  - Focuses attention on critical images
  - Keep explanation to a minimum.
  - Use your body for emphasis and focus.
  - Modulate volume and tone of voice.
  - Facial expression, gestures, posture, eye behavior
  - Orientation and space
  - Pauses and transitions

Identities and Identifications of the characters (Luke 10.31–35)

- Creating identities: make the key figures in the story *come to life* before your audience.
  - Describe the character so your audience can know them.
    - With words: mention the traits if the plot depends on it

- By what they say and how they say it
- Through their intentions and actions

  - Compare the various characters with one another.
  - Show how your character remains true to form or alters their behavior depending on the environment, test, and place.
  - Embody the "insides" of the character.
  - Use their name often.
  - Have them talk.
  - Act and talk as they act and talk.
  - Leave something to the imagination of your audience.

- Creating identifications: *constrain your audience to respond* to the figures and their traits.
  - With whom do you sympathize?
  - With whom do you resonate?
  - What characters do you find disgusting or revolting?
  - Whom do you admire?

Insights of the story (Luke 10.36)

- Discover the most important thing in the story (teaching, idea, theme, etc.).
- Explore the corollaries (outcomes or implications).
- *The insight question: what is it, above everything else, that this audience needs to know that this story embodies and reveals?*

Illuminations of the story (Luke 10.36)

- What do you see now that you did not see before you heard the story?
- How do you see differently what has always been here?

- *The illumination question: what is it, above everything else, that this story asks me to change in terms of my perspective on God, life, others, myself, or my world?*

- Changed the point of view and "tone of voice": No longer a storyteller, but "Thus says the Lord"

- The Word of God: Fill in all the cracks with the clear direct propositional Word of God after the Story of God.

Intersections, Implications, and re-Invitation of the audience to embrace the insight and illumination of the story (Luke 10.37)

- Make intersections between today's world and the story's world.
  - How does the story world illuminate our world today?
  - Where exactly do they tend to connect?
  - Explore implications for the world in which your audience lives.

- How do the characters and meanings integrate into their specific life situation?
  - How is the story world and its issues just like our own?
  - Invite your audience to embrace the story's insights and illuminations for their journey.

Conclusion

Can you begin to feel the excitement of this amazing tale of God's grace and love? In a world gone mad with power, lust, and greed, the Holy Spirit calls the Church to be faithful to God's biblical revelation of Jesus of Nazareth. This same clear, simple tale of God's awesome grace is recorded in the Bible, summarized in the creeds, and passed down faithfully through the centuries by the Church.

Despite the issues and challenges we face today in this world, this Story continues to draw the lost to its Good News. This great tale of Jesus of Nazareth, the Story's champion and hero, is as fresh today as when the disciples told it after the resurrection. Nothing has changed in the Story. The God who spawned it still loves us, the Savior who redeems us by his death still can save. The Spirit who fell on the first company of disciples can still empower us today. What then, do we need to do?

The answer is clear. We only need to hear this Story afresh, to sense its truthfulness and power once more, to recover the same true message that the consensus of the ancient Church fleshed out. The great traditions of Orthodoxy, Catholicism, Anglicanism, and the Protestant Reformation have defended it, artists have drawn it, musicians sung it, and missionaries brought it. All we need to do is rediscover it, and embody it once more.

Let us ask God to give us the courage to re-embrace this Narrative of narratives, this grand tale of God's matchless love. When all is said and done, it is a simple story after all. It can be understood through Scripture's testimony of creation, and seen in the great acts of God throughout the history of Israel. This great tale comes to its climax in the incarnation, death and resurrection of Jesus. Now, by faith, you can enter the Story, too.

If you look around, you won't fail to see many weird and fanciful competing master narratives seeking our allegiance. Religious jihad, political ideology, and strange philosophies all try to explain the meaning of the universe – where we came from and where we are going. For us who believe and follow Jesus of Nazareth, however, we need only hold onto the biblical Story.

This Story of God's saving acts in Christ for us is the narration of the entire universe. In its retelling, enactment, and embodiment, the truth about all things is made plain. All the big questions of life can be understood through the inspired telling of God's acts in history. Every time we go to church or Bible study or prayer meeting, we have an opportunity to rehearse the truth about God's great Story, and about his salvation in Jesus. You see, we are a continuation of the Story; we are that people who live out the Story in our confession, our songs and worship, our discipleship, and our testimony about Jesus. He is more than a tale; he is our very life and hope.

Prologue

· ·

From the Beginning to the Fullness of Time

Creation and the Fall

The Promise and the Patriarchs

Deliverance from Egypt

From Egypt to Canaan

The Promised Land

The Exile

The Remnant of Israel

Creation and the Fall

Eternity Past
1 Peter 1.18-21

Key Verse

2 Timothy 1.8-10

Therefore do not be ashamed of the testimony about our Lord, nor of me his prisoner, but share in suffering for the gospel by the power of God, who saved us and called us to a holy calling, not because of our works but because of his own purpose and grace, which he gave us in Christ Jesus before the ages began, and which now has been manifested through the appearing of our Savior Christ Jesus, who abolished death and brought life and immortality to light through the gospel.

In eternity past, God determined to send his Son to save a people from death

Theme Before creation, the Lord determined to send his Son to draw out of the earth a people for himself.

Setting Eternity past

Major Characters The eternal triune God

Plot

Introduction and Rising Action

1. From everlasting to everlasting the Lord is God.
2. The triune God, Father, Son, and Holy Spirit, has no beginning and no end.

Climax

3. Before the foundation of the world God determined to send his Son to draw out of the earth a people for himself.

Falling Action and Resolution

4. In the fullness of time, God's Son was revealed for us and our salvation.

Creation
Genesis 1-2

Key Verse

Genesis 1.26

*Then God said, "Let us make man in our image, after our likeness.
And let them have dominion over the fish of the sea and over the
birds of the heavens and over the livestock and over all the earth
and over every creeping thing that creeps on the earth."*

*In the beginning
God created the
heavens and
the earth*

Theme The Lord is king over all his creation, and he gives human beings dominion over the earth.

Setting The heavens and the earth

Major Characters
- Yahweh – the Eternal God, the Lord
- The first human pair

Plot

Introduction and Rising Action

1. In the beginning . . .
2. By his word, God speaks the heavens and the earth into existence.
3. The first three days the Lord forms the formless heavens and earth, making the sky, the sea, and dry land.
4. The second three days the Lord fills the void heavens and earth with the heavenly bodies, and creatures of all kinds.

Climax

5. On the sixth day, the Lord creates human beings in the image of God to rule and care for the earth.

Falling Action and Resolution

6. God rests on the seventh day as his work is finished, and it is all very good.

Adam and Eve in the Garden
Genesis 2.4-25

Key Verse

Genesis 2.7

. . . then the LORD God formed the man of dust from the ground and breathed into his nostrils the breath of life, and the man became a living creature.

The first human pair in the Garden of Eden

Christ foreshadowed (See note on page 41)

The Annunciation, p. 132

Theme | The Lord, the Creator, is the giver of all life and ruler of all that lives.

Setting | The Garden of Eden

Major Characters

- The Lord
- The man
- The woman

Plot

Introduction and Rising Action

1. The Lord forms the man out of the dirt of the earth and places him in the Garden of Eden.
2. The Lord forbids the man to eat from the tree of the knowledge of good and evil.
3. The Lord says that it is not good for the man to be alone.
4. God brings the animals in pairs and the man gives them names.

Climax

5. No match is found for him, so God causes a deep sleep to fall on the man.
6. He fashions woman out of the man's rib, as a suitable companion for him.

Falling Action and Resolution

7. The two human beings live in the Garden of Eden, working and tending it.
8. They are only forbidden to eat of the tree of the knowledge of good and evil.

The Serpent in the Garden
Genesis 3.1-7

Key Verse

Genesis 3.6

So when the woman saw that the tree was good for food, and that it was a delight to the eyes, and that the tree was to be desired to make one wise, she took of its fruit and ate, and she also gave some to her husband who was with her, and he ate.

The serpent tempts the woman

Christ foreshadowed
(See note on page 41)

The Temptation of Our Lord, *p. 154*

Theme The first human beings join the rebellion of the serpent, Satan, against God's kingdom reign.

Setting The Garden of Eden

Major Characters
- The serpent – Satan, the enemy of God
- The woman
- The man

Plot **Introduction and Rising Action**

1. The serpent is God's crafty enemy, Satan.
2. The serpent tempts the woman with the fruit from the forbidden tree of the knowledge of good and evil.

 Climax

3. In disobedience to God, the woman and the man listen to the serpent and eat.

Falling Action and Resolution

4. Their eyes are opened, and they realize they are naked.
5. They fashion garments for themselves out of fig leaves.

The Protoevangelium ("First Telling of the Gospel")
Genesis 3.8-21

Key Verse Genesis 3.15

"I will put enmity between you and the woman, and between your offspring and her offspring; he shall bruise your head, and you shall bruise his heel."

Theme ≫ The Lord will judge sin and rebellion against his Kingdom, but he promises to send a savior who will destroy the devil and deliver humanity from sin and death.

God promises a savior

Christ foreshadowed (See note on facing page)

The Return of Christ,
p. 244

Setting The Garden of Eden

Major Characters
- The Lord
- The serpent
- The woman
- The man

Plot

Introduction and Rising Action

1. After the disobedience of the first human pair, they hide themselves from God in fear and shame.
2. When the Lord comes to find them, he discovers that they have eaten the forbidden fruit.

Climax

3. The Lord pronounces a curse on the serpent, the woman, and the man.
4. Within his curse upon the serpent the Lord gives his first promise of redemption: the seed of the woman would come to crush the serpent's head, but the serpent would crush his heel.
5. The promise means that God would send a savior in the line of human beings who would defeat the devil and set humanity free, but who would suffer greatly in the process.
6. The curse upon th woman multiplies her pain in childbirth, and the curse upon the man increases the futility and difficulty of his labor.

Falling Action and Resolution

7. The man names his wife Eve, mother of all living.
8. The Lord graciously provides animal skins as clothing for the man and the woman.

This symbol represents a type of Christ in the Old Testament, foreshadowing some aspect of his person or work which Jesus of Nazareth would fulfill at his appearing. Jesus is the anti-type (i.e., the one to whom the type points and anticipates) of many of the objects, ceremonies, episodes, people, and events within the Old Testament. Truly, Jesus of Nazareth is the theme of the Bible (John 5.39-40; Luke 24.27, 44-48).

The Fall
Genesis 3.22-24

Key Verse

Romans 5.17

For if, because of one man's trespass, death reigned through that one man, much more will those who receive the abundance of grace and the free gift of righteousness reign in life through the one man Jesus Christ.

Theme 》

The great rebellion creates a rift between God and humanity, and subjects all things to death.

Adam and Eve are banished from the Garden

Setting | The Garden of Eden

Major Characters |
- The Lord
- The man and the woman
- Angels – guardians of the Tree of Life

Plot  | **Introduction and Rising Action**

1. The Lord determines to prevent humankind from accessing the tree of life and living forever.
2. As the Lord warned, eating the fruit subjected them and all creation to death.

 Climax

3. God banishes human beings from the Garden of Eden.
4. He sends them out of his presence, to the east.

 Falling Action and Resolution

5. He sets an angelic guard to prevent them from coming back.

6

Cain and Abel
Genesis 4.1-16

Key Verse

Genesis 4.7

"If you do well, will you not be accepted? And if you do not do well, sin is crouching at the door. Its desire is contrary to you, but you must rule over it."

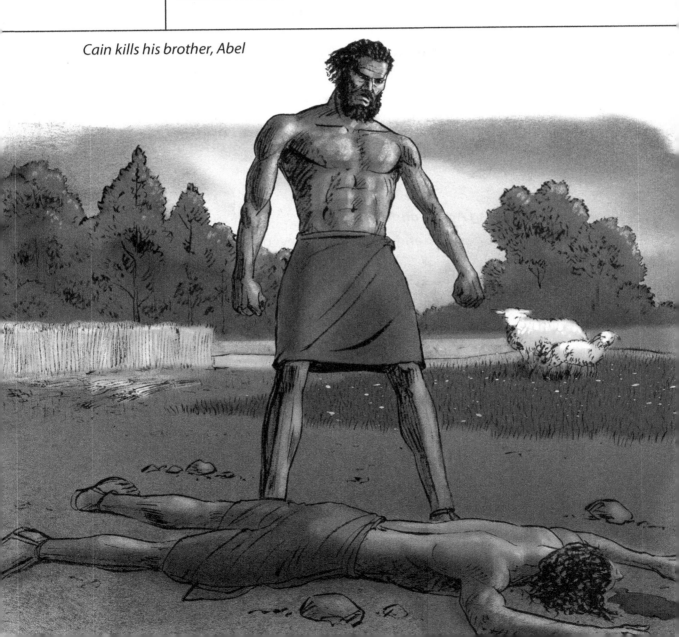

Cain kills his brother, Abel

Theme The Lord will judge sin and rebellion against his Kingdom, but he will show mercy to sinners.

Setting Fields near Adam and Eve's home

Major Characters

- Cain – Adam and Eve's first son
- Abel – Cain's younger brother
- The Lord

Plot

Introduction and Rising Action

1. Adam and Eve's first two sons are Cain and Abel.
2. Cain is a farmer, while Abel raises livestock.

Climax

3. One time when they both bring an offering to the Lord, Abel's offering is accepted by God, while Cain's offering is rejected.
4. In retaliation, Cain decides to murder Abel.
5. Cain invites his brother into a field and kills him.

Falling Action and Resolution

6. The Lord confronts Cain and says that he hears Abel's blood crying out from the ground.
7. The Lord banishes Cain to wander the earth but puts a mark on him so that no one would kill him.

The Flood
Genesis 6-9

Key Verse

Genesis 8.21

And when the LORD smelled the pleasing aroma, the LORD said in his heart, "I will never again curse the ground because of man, for the intention of man's heart is evil from his youth. Neither will I ever again strike down every living creature as I have done."

Theme ≫

The Lord will judge sin and rebellion against his Kingdom, but by his grace, he will rescue a remnant of humankind.

The ark weathers the flood

Christ foreshadowed (See note on page 41)

The Baptism of the Lord, p. 152

Setting

- The earth
- The ark
- Mount Ararat

Noah sends out a dove

Major Characters

- The Lord
- Noah
- Noah's family

Plot

Introduction and Rising Action

1. Humanity becomes so evil that God regrets that he made them.
2. He decides to flood the world and wipe it clean.
3. By grace, he chooses Noah and his family as the lone survivors.

Climax

4. He commands Noah to build a boat (the ark) that will house his family along with two of every kind of animal.
5. The Lord floods the world and every living thing dies except those in the ark.

Falling Action and Resolution

6. Once the rains stop, Noah sends out a dove to see if the ground is dried. When the dove brings back an olive branch, he unloads the ark.
7. God puts his rainbow in the sky with a promise that he will never again destroy all life with a flood.

Babel
Genesis 11.1-9

Key Verse

Genesis 11.9

Therefore its name was called Babel, because there the LORD confused the language of all the earth. And from there the LORD dispersed them over the face of all the earth.

"Let us build ourselves a city, and a tower with its top in the heavens."

Theme The Lord will judge sin and rebellion against his Kingdom, but he will fulfill his kingdom purposes in the world.

Setting The plains of Shinar

Major Characters
- Human beings
- The Lord

Plot

Introduction and Rising Action

1. The whole earth has one language.
2. They come together to build a city with a tower reaching into the heavens.

Climax

3. God looks down to see their tower.
4. He decides to confuse their speech to stop the building of the tower.

Falling Action and Resolution

5. No longer able to communicate, the people leave off building the tower.
6. Human beings are scattered across the earth with different languages. The place is named Babel.

The Promise and the Patriarchs

The Call of Abram
Genesis 12, 15

Key Verse

Genesis 12.2-3

"And I will make of you a great nation, and I will bless you and make your name great, so that you will be a blessing. I will bless those who bless you, and him who dishonors you I will curse, and in you all the families of the earth shall be blessed."

Genesis 15.6

And he believed the LORD, and he counted it to him as righteousness.

God makes a covenant with Abraham

Christ foreshadowed (See note on page 41)

The Annunciation, p. 132

The Calling of the Disciples, p. 156

Theme The Lord makes a covenant promise to bring the blessing of his Kingdom to the whole earth through the seed of Abraham.

Setting
- Haran – the city where Abraham's family has settled
- Canaan – the land God promises to give Abraham

Major Characters
- The Lord
- Abraham (called Abram in these stories)

Plot

Introduction and Rising Action

1. The Lord comes to Abram calls him to leave his home and go to a new land.
2. He promises to make him into a great nation, to bless him, and to through him to bless the whole world.

Climax

3. Abram obeys the Lord. He leaves Haran, with his wife Sarai and his nephew Lot, and journeys to Canaan.
4. The Lord confirms his promise to Abram, telling him his descendants will be as numerous as the stars in the sky.
5. Abram believes the Lord, and it is counted to him as righteousness.

Falling Action and Resolution

6. The Lord makes a covenant with Abram to give the land of Canaan to his descendants.

Melchizedek
Genesis 14.17-24

Key Verse

Genesis 14.19-20

And he blessed him and said, "Blessed be Abram by God Most High, Possessor of heaven and earth; and blessed be God Most High, who has delivered your enemies into your hand!" And Abram gave him a tenth of everything.

Melchizedek blesses Abram

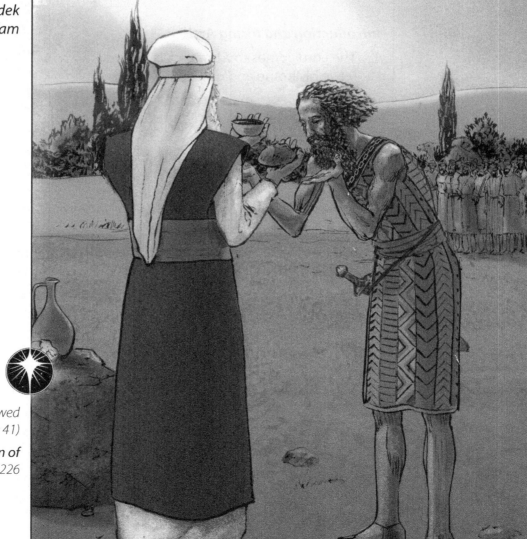

Christ foreshadowed (See note on page 41)

The Ascension of Christ, p. 226

Theme The Lord will appoint a king and priest to bless Abraham's descendants.

Setting The King's Valley in Canaan

Major Characters
- Abram
- Melchizedek – king of Salem (Jerusalem) in the land of Canaan

Plot

Introduction and Rising Action

1. Abram has just led a military campaign to rescue Lot from a group of five kings who had conquered Sodom.
2. After the victory, Melchizedek, king of Salem and priest of God, brings provisions for Abram's forces.

Climax

3. Melchizedek blesses Abram in the name of God.

Falling Action and Resolution

4. Abram gives Melchizedek one-tenth of all his goods.

Sodom and Gomorrah
Genesis 19

Key Verse

Genesis 19.15

As morning dawned, the angels urged Lot, saying, "Up! Take your wife and your two daughters who are here, lest you be swept away in the punishment of the city."

Lot flees Sodom with his family

Christ foreshadowed (See note on page 41)

The Ministry of John the Baptist, p. 136

Theme The Lord will judge sin and rebellion against his Kingdom, but he will show his covenant faithfulness to deliver his people.

Setting
- Sodom and Gomorrah – two wicked cities
- Zoar – the city where Lot flees to with his family

Major Characters
- Two angels
- Lot
- Lot's wife and daughters
- The men of Sodom

Plot

Introduction and Rising Action

1. The Lord sends two angels to investigate the evil of Sodom.
2. Lot invites the angels into his house to protect them from the wicked people of the city.

Climax

3. Because of God's love for Abraham, the angels warn Lot of the coming destruction and urge him to flee the city with his family.
4. Lot takes his wife and daughters and flees Sodom.

Falling Action and Resolution

5. As the angels are raining destruction on Sodom and Gomorrah, Lot's wife looks back and is turned into a pillar of salt.
6. Sodom and Gomorrah are completely destroyed.

God Tests Abraham
Genesis 22.1-19

Key Verse

Genesis 22.2

He said, "Take your son, your only son Isaac, whom you love, and go to the land of Moriah, and offer him there as a burnt offering on one of the mountains of which I shall tell you."

Abraham prepares to sacrifice Isaac

Christ foreshadowed (See note on page 41)

The Crucifixion: Jesus Carries His Cross, *p. 202*

Theme

The Lord will deliver his people and all peoples from sin and death by providing a sacrificial substitute.

Setting

The land of Moriah (and the road to Moriah)

Major Characters

- The Lord
- Abraham
- Isaac
- The Angel of the Lord

Plot

Introduction and Rising Action

1. The Lord calls Abraham to sacrifice his promised son, Isaac.
2. Abraham loads all the supplies for the sacrifice and sets out with Isaac and two servants.
3. Abraham and Isaac leave the servants and journey to the mountain alone for the sacrifice.
4. As they walk Isaac notices that they have not brought an animal for the sacrifice.

Climax

5. In obedience to the Lord, Abraham prepares to sacrifice Isaac, even taking the knife in his hand to kill the boy.
6. The Angel of the Lord intervenes and tells Abraham not to kill Isaac.

Falling Action and Resolution

7. Because of Abraham's willingness to sacrifice his son, the Lord affirms that he will absolutely fulfill his promise to bless Abraham and make him a great nation.

Joseph
Genesis 37, 45

Key Verse

Genesis 50.20

As for you, you meant evil against me, but God meant it for good, to bring it about that many people should be kept alive, as they are today.

Theme

The Lord will raise up a deliverer, who will be rejected by his people, but who will save them from death.

Setting

- The house of Jacob
- A field near Shechem
- Egypt

Joseph's brothers throw him in a pit and sell him as a slave

Christ foreshadowed (See note on page 41)

The Passion: Prayer in the Garden, p. 196

Major Characters

Joseph reveals his identity to his brothers

- Joseph – favorite son of a man who had twelve sons by four different women
- Jacob – Joseph's father
- The eleven other sons of Jacob – with a focus on Judah, Reuben, and Benjamin
- Potiphar – Joseph's master in Egypt
- Pharaoh – king of Egypt

Plot

Introduction and Rising Action

1. Jacob's favoritism and Joseph's dreams cause his brothers to hate Joseph.
2. The brothers sell Joseph into slavery and convince Jacob he is dead.
3. Joseph is sold in Egypt where he is put in charge of Potiphar's whole household. Potiphar's wife falsely accuses Joseph and he ends up in prison.
4. Joseph ascends to great power in Egypt when, from prison, he interprets the dreams of Pharaoh.

Climax

5. The dreams predict a great famine. When the famine comes, Joseph's brothers come to Egypt to buy grain from him.
6. Joseph tests his brothers to see if they have changed.

Falling Action and Resolution

7. He reveals of his identity to them and invites them to come to Egypt where he can provide for them.

Deliverance from Egypt

The Birth of Moses
Exodus 1-2

Key Verse

Exodus 2.10

When the child grew older, she brought him to Pharaoh's daughter, and he became her son. She named him Moses, "Because," she said, "I drew him out of the water."

Theme

The Lord will raise up a deliverer, who even as a baby will begin to save God's people from slavery and death.

Baby Moses in the Nile River

Setting
- Egypt under the rule of a Pharaoh who has forgotten about Joseph
- The Nile River

Major Characters
- Pharaoh
- Shiphrah and Puah – Hebrew midwives who save the baby boys from death
- The Levite and his wife – Moses's parents
- Moses – the baby

Plot

Introduction and Rising Action

1. A pharaoh arises in Egypt who does not remember Joseph, and who oppresses and enslaves the Israelites.

2. He gives an order that all male Hebrew babies should be put to death as soon as they are born.

3. Shiphrah and Puah, who serve as midwives to the Hebrew women, conspire to let the boys live.

Climax

4. A Levite and his wife have a baby boy. Three months after his birth they set in him adrift in a basket on the Nile River.

5. Pharaoh's daughter finds the baby and takes pity on him. She draws him out of the water.

6. Pharaoh's daughter unknowingly gives the baby back to his mother to be weaned.

Falling Action and Resolution

7. When he is weaned, the mother returns the baby to Pharaoh's daughter who names him Moses and raises him as her own.

The Plagues of Egypt
Exodus 3-11

Key Verse

Exodus 12.12

For I will pass through the land of Egypt that night, and I will strike all the firstborn in the land of Egypt, both man and beast; and on all the gods of Egypt I will execute judgments: I am the LORD.

Pharaoh holds his dead son

Theme The Lord will fight his enemies to save his people from slavery and death.

Setting
- The land of Midian
- In Egypt with the Israelites
- In Egypt with Pharaoh

Major Characters
- The Lord
- Moses – God's deliverer for his people
- Aaron – Moses's brother and spokesman
- Pharaoh – king of Egypt

Plot

Introduction and Rising Action

1. When the Israelites cry out for deliverance, the Lord calls Moses to lead the people out of Egypt, and Aaron to be his spokesman.
2. The Lord sends Moses to Pharaoh with a request to allow the people to leave Egypt and journey into the wilderness to celebrate a festival.
3. Pharaoh refuses to let the people go.

Climax

4. The Lord sends ten plagues on Egypt to demonstrate that he is God and to convince Pharaoh to let the Israelites go.
5. For the tenth plague, the Lord kills all of the firstborn sons of Egypt including Pharaoh's own son.

Falling Action and Resolution

6. Finally, Pharaoh lets Israel go.

The Passover
Exodus 12-13

Key Verse

Exodus 12.23

For the LORD will pass through to strike the Egyptians, and when he sees the blood on the lintel and on the two doorposts, the LORD will pass over the door and will not allow the destroyer to enter your houses to strike you.

The blood of
the lamb on
the doorpost

Christ foreshadowed
(See note on page 41)

The Crucifixion:
Jesus and the
Two Criminals,
p. 204

Theme The Lord will deliver his people from death through the blood of a sacrificial substitute.

Setting Egypt – on the night of the tenth plague

Major Characters
- The Lord
- Moses and Aaron
- Pharaoh

Plot

Introduction and Rising Action

1. On the night that he killed the firstborn children of Egypt, the Lord passed over the children of Israel in the land.
2. Each family is to slaughter a pure lamb and spread its blood on their door frames.
3. Wherever the Lord saw the blood, he would pass over that house.

Climax

4. Each Hebrew family smears the blood on their doors, eats the whole lamb and prepares to leave Egypt that night.
5. The Lord passes through and kills all of Egypt's firstborn children.
6. Pharaoh summons Moses and Aaron and demands that they and all the Israelites leave Egypt.

Falling Action and Resolution

7. The Lord commands his people to celebrate this great event with a yearly festival called Passover, where they would reenact this meal to remember his great deliverance.
8. God led his people out with a pillar of cloud by day and pillar of fire by night.

The Red Sea
Exodus 14-15

Key Verse

Exodus 14.13-14

And Moses said to the people, "Fear not, stand firm, and see the salvation of the LORD, which he will work for you today. For the Egyptians whom you see today, you shall never see again. The LORD will fight for you, and you have only to be silent."

Moses leads
Israel through
the Red Sea

Christ foreshadowed
(See note on page 41)

**The Baptism of
the Lord,** p. 152

Theme The Lord will fight his enemies to save his people from slavery and death.

Setting The Red Sea

Major Characters
- The Lord
- Moses
- Pharaoh and the Egyptian army
- The Israelites

Plot

Introduction and Rising Action

1. The Lord leads the Israelites to the shore of the Red Sea.
2. Pharaohs regrets letting the people go and leads his army to recapture them in the wilderness. He catches up to them at the shore of the Red Sea.
3. The Israelites are terrified of the army. Moses cries out to the Lord for help.

Climax

4. The Lord split the sea so that the Israelites could escape. The water formed a wall on either side, but they walked through on dry ground.
5. When Pharaoh pursues the Israelites into the sea, the Lord makes the water crash back in upon them and drown the whole army.

Falling Action and Resolution

6. Moses and the Israelites praise God with a song proclaiming the Lord's victory.

The Tabernacle
Exodus 40

Key Verse

Exodus 40.38

For the cloud of the LORD was on the tabernacle by day, and fire was in it by night, in the sight of all the house of Israel throughout all their journeys.

Theme >> The Lord will personally dwell among his people and lead them.

Setting The camp of Israel in the wilderness

Major Characters
- The Lord
- Moses
- Aaron and his sons

The tabernacle of the Lord

Plot

Introduction and Rising Action

1. After the great Exodus, the Lord met with his people to give them a Law.

2. He told them how they should live, and that they should build a tabernacle for his presence to be among them.

3. The tabernacle was a tent that could be set up and taken down easily as the Israelites journeyed through the wilderness.

4. The Lord gave specific requirements for the layout and design of the tabernacle.

5. The Lord set apart Aaron and his sons to serve as the priests.

Climax

6. Moses ensured that the tabernacle was completed exactly as the Lord has commanded.

7. The pillar of cloud and fire descended on the completed tabernacle.

Falling Action and Resolution

8. The Lord dwelt among his people and continued to lead them.

From Egypt to Canaan

19 The Twelve Spies
Numbers 13.1-14.10

Key Verse

Numbers 14.8-9

"If the LORD delights in us, he will bring us into this land and give it to us, a land that flows with milk and honey. Only do not rebel against the LORD. And do not fear the people of the land, for they are bread for us. Their protection is removed from them, and the LORD is with us; do not fear them."

The spies return from Canaan

Theme

The Lord will not give his victory and blessing to a faithless and disobedient people.

Setting

Kadesh-Barnea – the location of the Israelites camp on the southern edge of Canaan

Major Characters

- The Lord
- Moses
- Joshua
- Caleb
- The twelve spies

Plot

Introduction and Rising Action

1. After Israel left Sinai, the Lord led his people all the way to the border of Canaan, to an area called Kadesh-Barnea.

2. The Lord commands Moses to send a team of spies to see how good the land is, and what sort of people live in it. The report on the quality of the land is very positive. The produce they bring back to the camp is amazing.

3. The spies also see numerous large and strong people. They fear that Israel will not be able to defeat them in battle.

Climax

4. Two of the spies, Caleb and Joshua, try to persuade the people to trust the Lord and to not be afraid.

5. The nation refuses to enter the land and take it.

Falling Action and Resolution

6. They hatch a plan to choose a new leader and return to Egypt.

7. The whole congregation of the people threatens to kill Moses, Caleb, and Joshua.

20 | *Wilderness Wanderings*
Numbers 14.11-45

Key Verse | Numbers 14.22-23

. . . none of the men who have seen my glory and my signs that I did in Egypt and in the wilderness, and yet have put me to the test these ten times and have not obeyed my voice, shall see the land that I swore to give to their fathers. And none of those who despised me shall see it.

Israel wanders in the wilderness

*Christ foreshadowed
(See note on page 41)*

**The Temptation of
Our Lord**, p. 154

Theme The Lord will judge sin and rebellion against his kingdom, even among his covenant people.

Setting Kadesh Barnea – an area on the south end of the land of Canaan

Major Characters
- The Lord
- Moses
- Aaron
- Caleb and Joshua
- The Israelites
- The inhabitants of Canaan

Plot

Introduction and Rising Action

1. In response to the rebellion at Kadesh Barnea, the Lord says that he is going to destroy the entire nation except for Moses, Joshua, Caleb, and Aaron.

2. Moses intercedes for the people and prays for the Lord to forgive them.

Climax

3. The Lord condemns the people to wander in the desert for forty years until every adult who refused to enter the land dies off.

4. Once the people hear this, they change their mind and decide to attack the Canaanites.

5. The Canaanites defeat them easily.

Falling Action and Resolution

6. For the next forty years, the pillar of cloud and fire leads the people all around the wilderness.

Crossing the Jordan
Joshua 3-4

Key Verse

Joshua 3.7

The LORD said to Joshua, "Today I will begin to exalt you in the sight of all Israel, that they may know that, as I was with Moses, so I will be with you."

Theme

The Lord's people will remember and reenact his mighty saving deeds.

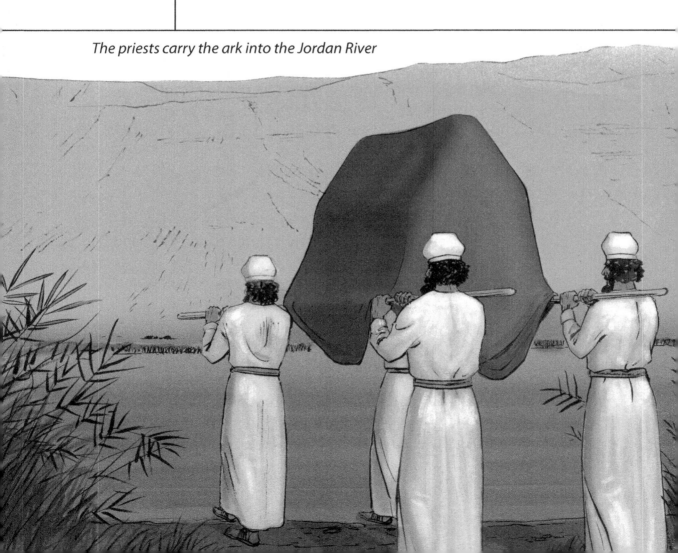

The priests carry the ark into the Jordan River

Setting   The Jordan River – the eastern edge of the land of Canaan

Major Characters

- The Lord
- Joshua
- The priests – carriers of the Ark of the Covenant
- The Israelites – a new generation after forty years in the wilderness

Plot

Introduction and Rising Action

1. After forty years wandering in the wilderness, the Lord anoints Joshua to lead a new generation into the land of Canaan.
2. They come to the east side of Canaan and encounter the Jordan River.
3. The Lord tells Joshua that just as the Israelites followed Moses through the Red Sea, so they would follow his through the Jordan.

Climax

4. The priests carrying the Ark of the Covenant step foot in the river and the water stop flowing.
5. With the waters piling up in a heap, the Israelites cross the river on dry land.

Falling Action and Resolution

6. They set up two monuments of twelve stones to remember this great event. One they set up in the river itself where the priests stood.
7. For the second monument they took twelve stones from the dry riverbed and set them up at their camp in Gilgal. The stones were there to help the people remember the deeds of the Lord and tell the story to their children.

Winning Canaan
Joshua 5.13-6.27

Key Verse

Joshua 6.20

So the people shouted, and the trumpets were blown. As soon as the people heard the sound of the trumpet, the people shouted a great shout, and the wall fell down flat, so that the people went up into the city, every man straight before him, and they captured the city.

Joshua leads the victory over Jericho

Theme The Lord will give victory through the faith and obedience of his people.

Setting Jericho – a major city in the eastern part of Canaan

Major Characters
- The Lord
- Joshua
- The Israelite army

Plot

Introduction and Rising Action

1. Israel camps near Jericho and prepares to attack it.
2. The commander of the Lord's army meets with Joshua to reassure him that God is indeed with his people.
3. Jericho is protected by stone walls that were high and thick. It would be very difficult for an invading army to take such a city.

Climax

4. The Lord tells the people to march around the city for seven days.
5. Israel obeys the plan laid out by the Lord and, on the seventh day, the great walls of Jericho come crashing down.

Falling Action and Resolution

6. The Lord also commands that Rahab the prostitute be spared from the destruction of the city because of her help for the spies Joshua had sent (See Joshua 2 for this story).

The Promised Land

Gideon
Judges 6-7

Key Verse 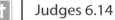 Judges 6.14

And the LORD turned to him and said, "Go in this might of yours and save Israel from the hand of Midian; do not I send you?"

Gideon asks the Lord for a sign

Theme The Lord will deliver not by the might of armies and the courage of leaders, but by the victory of faith.

Setting

- Gideon's winepress
- Gideon's hometown
- Gideon's army camp

Major Characters

- The Lord
- Gideon
- Gideon's army

Plot

Introduction and Rising Action

1. After the Israelites enter the land, they do not stay faithful to the Lord. The Lord allows their enemies to defeat them, but he raises up judges to deliver them.

2. When the Midianites defeat Israel, the Lord calls Gideon, who is treading out grain in his winepress.

3. Gideon repeatedly asks the Lord for signs to confirm the word of the Lord.

4. When the Lord calls Gideon to destroy the altar of Baal in his hometown.

Climax

5. Before he leads the army out to fight the Midianites, Gideon twice asks the Lord to confirm his word through a sign with a fleece. The Lord confirms his word.

6. He pares Gideon's army down from 32,000 to 300.

Falling Action and Resolution

7. With the 300, the Lord delivers Israel from Midian.

Samson
Judges 16

Key Verse

Judges 16.28

Then Samson called to the LORD and said, "O Lord GOD, please remember me and please strengthen me only this once, O God, that I may be avenged on the Philistines for my two eyes."

Samson brings down the walls on the Philistines

Theme	The Lord will be faithful to his promise, even when his people are faithless.

Setting

- The Valley of Sorek – home of Delilah
- Gaza – a major Philistine city

Major Characters

- Samson
- Delilah
- The Philistines

Plot

Introduction and Rising Action

1. Samson has amazing strength. He is a Nazirite from his birth. So long as he keeps his vows (one of which is not cutting his hair).

2. He falls in love with Delilah, and the Philistine lords pressure her to find out the secret of Samson's great strength.

3. Samson eventually tells Delilah that he will lose his strength if his hair is cut.

Climax

4. She cuts his hair and binds him for the Philistines to capture him.

5. The Philistines gouge out Samson's eyes and imprison him.

6. At a great gathering, the Philistines bring out Samson to entertain the crowd.

Falling Action and Resolution

7. Samson asks the Lord for one last act of great strength. He pushes down the pillars of the building and all of the Philistines present are killed in the collapse.

Saul
1 Samuel 8-10 (10.17-24)

Key Verse

1 Samuel 10.19

"But today you have rejected your God, who saves you from all your calamities and your distresses, and you have said to him, 'Set a king over us.' Now therefore present yourselves before the LORD by your tribes and by your thousands."

Theme The Lord will anoint a human king to rule his people.

Setting
- The Land of Zuph
- Gibeah
- Mizpah

Samuel proclaims Saul king

Major Characters

- The Lord
- Samuel – prophet of the Lord
- Saul – son of Kish, a Benjamite
- The Israelites

Plot

Introduction and Rising Action

1. The Israelites demand a king like the other nations around them.
2. The Lord grants their request and sends to Samuel to anoint Saul.
3. Saul is a head taller than anyone else in Israel.

Climax

4. Samuel first anoints Saul secretly in the land of Zuph. Saul is out looking for his father's lost donkeys. The Lord directs Samuel to anoint his king.
5. On his return trip, Saul meets a group of prophets in Gibeah. The Spirit of God possesses him and he begins to prophesy with them.

Falling Action and Resolution

6. At Mizpah, Samuel calls all Israel to come before him so that a king can be chosen.
7. Saul's family is chosen by lot, but Saul is hiding among the baggage. When he is found, Samuel presents him to the people as their king.

26

Tearing Samuel's Robe
1 Samuel 15.10-35

Key Verse

1 Samuel 15.22

And Samuel said, "Has the LORD as great delight in burnt offerings and sacrifices, as in obeying the voice of the LORD? Behold, to obey is better than sacrifice, and to listen than the fat of rams."

Theme »

The Lord's king will be completely faithful and obedient.

The kingdom ripped away from Saul

Setting | Mt. Carmel

Major Characters

- The Lord
- Samuel
- Saul

Plot

Introduction and Rising Action

1. Samuel explains to Saul that he is to attack and completely destroy the Amalekites, not taking any spoils for himself.
2. Saul attacks and defeats the Amalekites, but takes the best of the spoils, and allows King Agag to live.
3. The Lord tells Samuel what is happening. He says that he regrets making Saul king, and the he will give the kingdom to another.

Climax

4. Samuel confronts Saul at Carmel.
5. Saul tries to explain that he was keeping the spoils as a sacrifice for the Lord.
6. Samuel says the Lord desires obedience rather than sacrifice.

Falling Action and Resolution

7. As Samuel turns to leave, Saul grabs his robe and it rips. Samuels says that in the same way, the Lord will rip the kingdom from Saul's hand. Samuel then kills Agag himself.

David Is Anointed
1 Samuel 16.1-13

Key Verse

1 Samuel 16.7

But the LORD said to Samuel, "Do not look on his appearance or on the height of his stature, because I have rejected him. For the LORD sees not as man sees: man looks on the outward appearance, but the LORD looks on the heart."

Samuel anoints David as the new king

*Christ foreshadowed
(See note on page 41)*

Theme The Lord's anointed king will be chosen not for his appearance but for his heart.

Setting Bethlehem – the hometown of David

Major Characters

- The Lord
- Samuel
- Jesse
- Eliab
- David

Plot

Introduction and Rising Action

1. The Lord sends Samuel to the house of Jesse, the Bethlehemite to anoint a new king in place of Saul.
2. Samuel invites Jesse's whole family to a sacrifice.
3. Samuel is impressed by Jesse's first son, Eliab, and believes that surely he is the one to be the next king.
4. The Lord tells Samuel that he is not looking at the man's appearance but this heart.

Climax

5. Jesse made seven of his sons pass before Samuel, but the Lord did not choose any of them.
6. When Samuel hears that there is another son out keeping the sheep, he tells them to bring him.

Falling Action and Resolution

7. Samuel anoints David, the youngest son of Jesse, as the next king of Israel.

David and Goliath
1 Samuel 17

Key Verse

1 Samuel 17.46-47

"This day the LORD will deliver you into my hand, and I will strike you down and cut off your head. And I will give the dead bodies of the host of the Philistines this day to the birds of the air and to the wild beasts of the earth, that all the earth may know that there is a God in Israel, and that all this assembly may know that the LORD saves not with sword and spear. For the battle is the LORD's, and he will give you into our hand."

David fights the giant Goliath

Theme The Lord's anointed king will defeat the enemy and deliver God's people from slavery not by physical might but by faith in the Lord.

Setting Socoh – A field of battle between the Philistines and Israelites

Major Characters

- Goliath
- Saul
- David
- The Israelite army

Plot

Introduction and Rising Action

1. Goliath, the gigantic Philistine champion, challenges Israel to send forth a man for individual combat.
2. Saul, along with the whole army of Israel, is terrified of Goliath.
3. David arrives with provision for his brothers who are in the army.

Climax

4. When he hears the challenge of Goliath he is ready to fight him.
5. Saul tries to outfit David with his armor, but David takes only five smooth stones and a slingshot to fight the giant.
6. After declaring that the battle belongs to the Lord, David kills Goliath.

Falling Action and Resolution

7. David then leads Israel in a rout of the Philistines.

29

Solomon
1 Kings 3

Key Verse

1 Kings 3.12

. . . behold, I now do according to your word. Behold, I give you a wise and discerning mind, so that none like you has been before you and none like you shall arise after you.

Solomon gives a wise judgment

Theme The Lord's king will reign with God's wisdom, ruling in righteousness and dispensing justice.

Setting
- Gibeon where Solomon went to offer a sacrifice
- Jerusalem

Major Characters
- The Lord
- Solomon
- The two mothers

Plot

Introduction and Rising Action

1. The Lord comes to Solomon and offers to give him whatever he asks.
2. Solomon asks for the wisdom to rule God's people well.
3. The Lord grants Solomon's request by making him wiser than any other person, and also grants him power, wealth, and victory.

Climax

4. Solomon demonstrates this great wisdom in deciding a tough case between two mothers.
5. One mother accuses the other of switching their babies in the night after her own has died.
6. Solomon decides that the baby should be cut in two and half given to each woman. One woman accepts the decision, but the child's true mother begs for the boy to live.

Falling Action and Resolution

7. Solomon's wise decision revealed the truth of the matter.

Solomon's Temple
1 Kings 8

Key Verse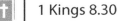

1 Kings 8.30

And listen to the plea of your servant and of your people Israel, when they pray toward this place. And listen in heaven your dwelling place, and when you hear, forgive.

Solomon's
Temple for
the Lord

Theme | The Lord will be present with his people in a temple, through the sacrifice of a priest.

Setting | Jerusalem – the site of the Temple in Jerusalem

Major Characters

- The Lord
- Solomon
- The elders and priests of Israel

Plot

Introduction and Rising Action

1. Solomon builds a temple for the Lord and brings the Ark of the Covenant into the holy of holies.

Climax

2. Just as he did for Moses and the tabernacle, the Lord shows his presence by a thick cloud the will not allow anyone to enter the temple for a time.
3. Solomon offers a prayer of dedication for the temple.
4. Then he blesses the assembly and charges them to keep the law of the Lord.
5. He offers thousands and thousands of sacrifices to dedicate the temple.

Falling Action and Resolution

6. Israel held a great festival to celebrate the building and dedication of the temple.
7. Solomon then dismissed the people to go home in the joy of the Lord.

The Exile

Elijah
1 Kings 18.1-40

Key Verse

1 Kings 18.38-39

Then the fire of the LORD fell and consumed the burnt offering and the wood and the stones and the dust, and licked up the water that was in the trench. And when all the people saw it, they fell on their faces and said, "The LORD, he is God; the LORD, he is God."

Elijah calls down fire from heaven

Theme The Lord is the only true and living God, and his people will worship him alone.

Setting Mt. Carmel

Major Characters

- Elijah – the prophet of the Lord
- Obadiah – a godly palace attendant
- Ahab – wicked king of Israel
- 450 prophets of Baal

Plot

Introduction and Rising Action

1. Three years into a drought, the Lord calls Elijah to return to Israel and confront Ahab.

2. Obadiah, who is faithful to the Lord, meets Elijah and goes to tell Ahab where he is.

3. Elijah confronts Ahab and sets up a contest. He asks that the prophets of Baal and Asherah meet him on Mount Carmel. The contest is to see whose God will answer when called.

Climax

4. The prophets of Baal and Asherah call on their gods for several hours, but nothing happens.

5. Then Elijah sets up his sacrifice. He calls for several gallons of water to be poured over the offering.

6. The Lord answers in spectacular fashion by consuming not only the sacrifice, but all the water that Elijah had poured over it as well.

Falling Action and Resolution

7. The people respond with repentance, declaring that the Lord is the true God. Elijah then commands that the prophets of the false gods be put to death.

Elisha
2 Kings 6.8-23

Key Verse

2 Kings 6.16-17

He said, "Do not be afraid, for those who are with us are more than those who are with them." Then Elisha prayed and said, "O LORD, please open his eyes that he may see." So the LORD opened the eyes of the young man, and he saw, and behold, the mountain was full of horses and chariots of fire all around Elisha.

The Lord opens the eyes of Elisha's servant

Theme The Lord of heavens armies will fight for his servants and conquer his enemies.

Setting

- Aram
- Dothan – home of Elisha
- Samaria – home of the king of Israel

Major Characters

- The king of Aram
- Elisha
- Elisha's servant
- The king of Israel

Plot

Introduction and Rising Action

1. When the king of Aram finds out that Elisha has been thwarting his plans by revealing them to the king of Israel, he sends his army to Dothan to seize Elisha.
2. Elisha's servant is terrified when he wakes up in the morning to find the Aramean army around the city.

Climax

3. Elisha prays that the Lord would open his servant's eyes. He then sees that the hills are full of angelic armies all around.
4. Elisha prays that the Aramean army would be struck blind.
5. He leads the blinded army to Samaria where he prays again to restore their vision.

Falling Action and Resolution

6. The king of Israel wants to kill them, but Elisha says they should be treated well.
7. After feeding the army, he sent them back to Aram. The Arameans no longer raided or attacked Israel.

Jonah
Jonah 1-4

Key Verse

Jonah 3.10

When God saw what they did, how they turned from their evil way, God relented of the disaster that he had said he would do to them, and he did not do it.

Jonah is thrown overboard

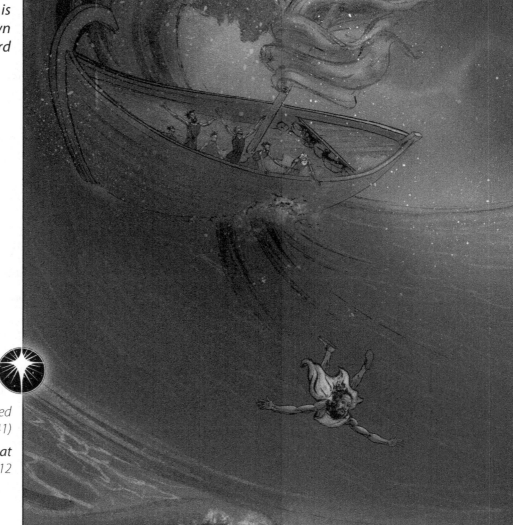

Christ foreshadowed
(See note on page 41)

The Guards at the Tomb, p. 212

Theme The Lord will accept anyone who repents and turns to him in faith, he desires that none should perish.

Setting
- Joppa
- A ship to Tarshish
- Nineveh

Major Characters
- The Lord
- Jonah
- The sailors
- The Ninevites

Plot

Introduction and Rising Action

1. The Lord calls Jonah to go preach to Nineveh, but Jonah flees the opposite direction. In the port of Joppa, he boards a ship for Tarshish.

2. The ship is caught up in a terrible storm. The sailors cast lots and find the Jonah is the cause of the storm. They throw him into the sea and the storm stops.

3. The Lord appoints a big fish to swallow Jonah. From the fish's belly Jonah cries out for mercy.

Climax

4. After three days, the Lord causes the fish to spit out Jonah on the shore.

5. The Lord calls Jonah to Nineveh a second time and Jonah obeys. He goes and preaches to the Ninevites.

6. Jonah's preaching inspires a great repentance in Nineveh and the Lord relents from the destruction he had planned.

Falling Action and Resolution

7. Jonah is angry that the Lord spares Nineveh. The Lord gives Jonah an object lesson with a plant and tells him that he cares for Nineveh.

The Captivity
2 Chronicles 36

Key Verse

2 Chronicles 36.15-16

The LORD, the God of their fathers, sent persistently to them by his messengers, because he had compassion on his people and on his dwelling place. But they kept mocking the messengers of God, despising his words and scoffing at his prophets, until the wrath of the LORD rose against his people, until there was no remedy.

God's people taken into captivity

*Christ foreshadowed
(See note on page 41)*

***The Guards at
the Tomb***, p. 212

Theme The Lord will judge the sin and rebellion of his people, but he will not forsake his covenant promise.

Setting
- Jerusalem
- Babylon
- Persia

Major Characters
- The Lord
- The final kings of Judah
- Nebuchadnezzar – King of Babylon
- Jeremiah
- Cyrus – King of Persia

Plot

Introduction and Rising Action

1. The final kings of Israel are all evil.
2. The sin of Judah becomes so great that the Lord brings his wrath against them.

Climax

3. He allows Nebuchadnezzar, king of Babylon (also called the Chaldeans) to conquer them and take them into exile.
4. The capital city of Jerusalem and the temple are completely destroyed, the people are either killed in the battle or taken into exile in Babylon hundreds of miles away.
5. The prophet Jeremiah is the Lord's messenger sent during this time to interpret the events of the exile for the people.

Falling Action and Resolution

6. However, the Lord had promised that his people would return to their land.
7. Under the rule of King Cyrus of Persia, the exiles are allowed to return to Judah.

35 The Valley of Dry Bones
Ezekiel 37.1-14

Key Verse

Ezekiel 37.14

"And I will put my Spirit within you, and you shall live, and I will place you in your own land. Then you shall know that I am the LORD; I have spoken, and I will do it, declares the LORD."

Theme

The Lord will send his Spirit to bring new life to his people who are dead in sin.

Ezekiel's vision of the valley of dry bones

Christ foreshadowed (See note on page 41)

The Coming of the Holy Spirit, p. 230

Setting A prophetic vision (during the Exile)

Major Characters
- The Lord
- Ezekiel
- The dry bones

Plot

Introduction and Rising Action

1. The Lord shows Ezekiel a vision of a valley full of dry bones.
2. He asks Ezekiel if they can live.
3. He then calls Ezekiel to prophesy life to the bones.

Climax

4. As he speaks, the bones begin to join together, and muscles, and flesh return to them
5. The Lord then calls Ezekiel to prophesy to the breath, telling it to come and make them live again.
6. As he spoke, the people in the valley came to life and stood as a great multitude.

Falling Action and Resolution

7. The Lord explains that this is what he will do for his people. He will bring them out of their graves and put his Spirit in them that they may live.

36 | We Will Not Bow
Daniel 3

Key Verse

Daniel 3.17-18

"If this be so, our God whom we serve is able to deliver us from the burning fiery furnace, and he will deliver us out of your hand, O king. But if not, be it known to you, O king, that we will not serve your gods or worship the golden image that you have set up."

The three Hebrew boys in the fiery furnace

Theme The Lord will stand with his servants to deliver them from the hands of the wicked.

Setting The Plain of Dura in Babylon (Israel in Exile)

Major Characters
- Shadrach, Meshach, and Abednego
- Nebuchadnezzar

Plot

Introduction and Rising Action

1. Nebuchadnezzar sets up a golden statue and orders everyone in Babylon to fall down and worship.
2. Three Hebrews, Shadrach, Meshach, and Abednego, refuse to worship the statue.
3. Nebuchadnezzar is enraged and brings them in to question them.

Climax

4. Shadrach, Meshach, and Abednego refuse to bow down, choosing instead to be thrown into a fiery furnace.
5. Nebuchadnezzar turns the heat up to seven times normal and throws them in. When he goes to look in, he sees four men instead of three in the fire.

Falling Action and Resolution

6. He calls Shadrach, Meshach, and Abednego out of the fire. When they come out they are not burned or hurt.
7. Nebuchadnezzar forbids anyone in his kingdom from blaspheming against the Lord because of his great deliverance.

Daniel
Daniel 6

Key Verse

Daniel 6.26-27

"I make a decree, that in all my royal dominion people are to tremble and fear before the God of Daniel, for he is the living God, enduring forever; his kingdom shall never be destroyed, and his dominion shall be to the end. He delivers and rescues; he works signs and wonders in heaven and on earth, he who has saved Daniel from the power of the lions."

Daniel in the lions' den

Christ foreshadowed
(See note on page 41)

Paul, Ambassador in Chains, p. 236

Theme
The Lord will stand with his servants to deliver them from the hands of the wicked.

Setting
The kingdom of the Medes and Persians (formerly Babylon)

Major Characters
- King Darius
- Daniel
- Government officials – satraps and high officials under Darius

Plot

Introduction and Rising Action

1. Daniel excels as a government official and makes the other officials jealous.
2. In a plot against Daniel, some the government officials convince Darius to make a decree that anyone who prays to someone other than the king should be thrown into the lion's den.
3. When Daniel hears of the decree, he continues to pray three times a day to the Lord.

Climax

4. Although Darius is grieved, the officials hold him to his decree. He throws Daniel into the lion's den.
5. In the morning when Darius rushes to check on Daniel, he finds him alive and well. The Lord sent angel to shut the mouths of the lions.

Falling Action and Resolution

6. Darius removes Daniel from the lion's den and praises the Lord.
7. He throws the officials that had conspired against Daniel into the lion's den, and they are immediately torn apart by the lions.

The Remnant of Israel

Rebuilding the Temple
Ezra 3-6

Key Verse

Ezra 5.1-2

Now the prophets, Haggai and Zechariah the son of Iddo, prophesied to the Jews who were in Judah and Jerusalem, in the name of the God of Israel who was over them. Then Zerubbabel the son of Shealtiel and Jeshua the son of Jozadak arose and began to rebuild the house of God that is in Jerusalem, and the prophets of God were with them, supporting them.

Theme

The Lord will build a new temple where his people will worship him spirit and in truth.

Setting

Jerusalem

Rebuilding the Temple

Major Characters

- Jeshua – priest of the Lord
- Zerubbabel – a leader of God's people
- Haggai and Zechariah – prophets of the Lord
- King Darius

Plot

Introduction and Rising Action

1. After Babylon falls to Persia, King Cyrus allows the Jewish people return to Jerusalem.
2. Their first work is to rebuild the temple.

Climax

3. They lay the foundation, but then they face opposition from neighboring peoples.
4. Zerubbabel and Jeshua lead the people to continue building in the face of the opposition.
5. The prophets Haggai and Zechariah urged the people on by prophesying in the name of the Lord.

Falling Action and Resolution

6. King Darius issues a decree that all the opposition to the Jews should cease, and that everything they need should be provided for them.
7. They complete and dedicate the second temple, and celebrate the Passover festival that year.

39 Rebuilding the Walls
Nehemiah 1-8

Key Verse

Nehemiah 2.17

Then I said to them, "You see the trouble we are in, how Jerusalem lies in ruins with its gates burned. Come, let us build the wall of Jerusalem, that we may no longer suffer derision."

Rebuilding the walls of Jerusalem

Theme | The Lord will build a new Jerusalem where his people will dwell in peace.

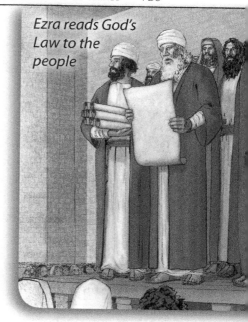

Ezra reads God's Law to the people

Setting

- Susa – capital of Persia
- Jerusalem

Major Characters

- King Artaxerxes of Persia
- Nehemiah
- Sanaballat and Tobiah – enemies of the Jews
- Ezra

Plot

Introduction and Rising Action

1. Nehemiah is a cup-bearer for King Artaxerxes. When he hears of Jerusalem's poor condition he mourns, fasts, and prays.
2. He asks the king for leave and assistance to go repair the walls of Jerusalem.

Climax

3. The Lord gives Nehemiah favor with the king of Persia. Nehemiah returns and leads the people rebuild the wall around Jerusalem.
4. Sanballat and Tobiah are enemies of God's people who oppose the work on the walls. Their violent opposition slows but does not stop the building.
5. The wall is completed under Nehemiah's supervision.

Falling Action and Resolution

6. Ezra, a scribe, reads the Law for the people.
7. When the people are grieved by hearing the Law, he tells them that the joy of the Lord is their strength and calls for celebration.

Queen Esther
Esther 3-8

Key Verse Esther 4.14

"For if you keep silent at this time, relief and deliverance will rise for the Jews from another place, but you and your father's house will perish. And who knows whether you have not come to the kingdom for such a time as this?"

Theme ≫ The Lord's deliverer will save God's people through self-sacrifice.

Esther approaches the King of Persia

Setting   The Citadel of Susa

Major Characters

- King Ahasuerus (Xerxes)
- Esther
- Mordecai
- Haman

Plot

Introduction and Rising Action

1. Esther becomes queen of Persia when the former queen is deposed.
2. Haman is an exalted servant of the king. Mordecai, Esther's uncle, refuses to bow down before Haman.
3. Haman, out of hatred for Mordecai, persuades the king to order the annihilation of the Jews.

Climax

4. Mordecai asks Esther to talk to the king about saving the Jews. Esther is afraid to go in before the king uninvited, but Mordecai tells her that it may be for this very time that she has been put in her position as queen.
5. Esther risks her own life to save the Jews by exposing Haman's evil plot.

Falling Action and Resolution

6. Haman dies on the very gallows where he had intended to hang Mordecai.
7. The Jews are delivered by a second kingly decree, warning them of the plot and urging them to defend themselves.

The Prophetic Promise
Isaiah 11.1-9

Key Verse

Isaiah 11.2

And the Spirit of the LORD shall rest upon him, the Spirit of wisdom and understanding, the Spirit of counsel and might, the Spirit of knowledge and the fear of the LORD.

Theme

The Lord will send Messiah, a new king full of the Holy Spirit who will bring the blessing of God's Kingdom to all creation.

"Thus says the Lord . . ."

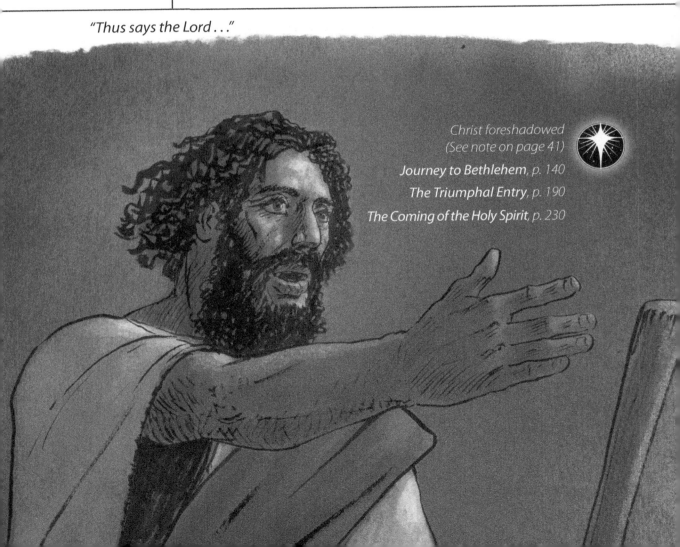

Christ foreshadowed
(See note on page 41)
Journey to Bethlehem, p. 140
The Triumphal Entry, p. 190
The Coming of the Holy Spirit, p. 230

Setting A prophetic word

Major Characters
- Isaiah the Prophet
- Messiah – the coming King
- The Spirit of the Lord

Plot

Introduction and Rising Action

1. Isaiah, along with all the Law and the Prophets, predict the coming of Messiah, the king of God's kingdom.
2. He says a shoot will come from the stump of Jesse. The coming king will be born in the line of David.

Climax

3. The Spirit of God will rest on the King.
4. The King will fear the Lord, ruling with justice and righteousness.
5. He will usher in the age of God's Kingdom where violence and death are no more.
6. He will bring the knowledge of the Lord across the whole earth.

Falling Action and Resolution

7. The whole Old Testament builds anticipation for this one who would come and reign forever . . .

The Story of God in Christ

. . . .

The Fullness of Time

Advent

Christmas

Epiphany

Lent

Holy Week

The Resurrection of Christ

The Ascension of Christ

Pentecost

Kingdomtide

Advent

. . . .

The Coming of Christ

Advent joyously affirms the First and Second Comings of our Lord.
Through the prophets, God foretold the Messiah's appearing to his people, Israel.
Through the angels, he announced his birth to Zechariah, Mary, and the shepherds.
Let us reverently ponder the sure promise of God – the Deliverer will come
and ransom captive Israel and the world.

The Annunciation
Luke 1.26-38

Key Verse

Luke 1.31

And behold, you will conceive in your womb and bear a son, and you shall call his name Jesus.

Theme

The Lord announces the arrival of his Messiah, a son of David, to establish his Kingdom.

Setting

Nazareth – a small town in northern Israel

Major Characters

- Mary – a young woman of Nazareth
- Gabriel – the angel

Plot

Introduction and Rising Action

1. Mary is a young woman living in Nazareth. She is an unmarried virgin.

2. The Lord sends the angel Gabriel to announce to Mary that, though she is a virgin, she will conceive a child and name him Jesus.

3. This child will be the Son of God and the Lord will give him the throne of David and kingdom that will never end.

The Angel Gabriel visits the Virgin Mary to announce the arrival of the Messiah

Climax

4. Mary asks how this is possible since she is a virgin.

5. The angel explains that the child would be conceived by the Holy Spirit.

6. He also tells Mary that her relative, Elizabeth has also conceived a child in her old age.

Falling Action and Resolution

7. Mary says she is the servant of the Lord and accepts the word of the angel.

8. The angel departs.

Old Testament Foundation: The Promise of a Savior

The Promise to Adam and Eve, Genesis 3.15 (p. 36)

The seed of the woman: Messiah is born of a woman, a "daughter of Eve" in C.S. Lewis's terms.

The Promise to Abraham, Genesis 12.1-3, 15.5 (p. 52)

The seed of Abraham: Messiah is a descendant of Abraham, Isaac, and Jacob, an heir of God's promise and blessing.

The Covenant with David, 2 Samuel 7.11-16

The Son of David: Messiah is born in the family of David, the line of God's covenant king.

43 The Visitation
Luke 1.39-56

Key Verse

Luke 1.46-47

And Mary said, "My soul magnifies the Lord, and my spirit rejoices in God my Savior."

Theme

The Lord gives his servants joy by confirming the arrival of Messiah.

Elizabeth receives Mary, the mother of the Messiah

Setting A Judean town in the hill country – the house of Zechariah and Elizabeth

Major Characters

- Mary
- Elizabeth
- The babies of Mary and Elizabeth

Plot

Introduction and Rising Action

1. After the visitation of Gabriel, Mary goes to visit her relative Elizabeth.
2. When Mary arrives, the baby in Elizabeth's womb leaps for joy.

Climax

3. Elizabeth greets Mary with a blessing.
4. She tells Mary of her baby leaping in her womb and blesses her for believing the Lord.

Falling Action and Resolution

5. Mary responds with a beautiful hymn of praise (often called The Magnificat).
6. Mary remains with Elizabeth for three months.

The Ministry of John the Baptist
Matthew 3.1-12

Key Verse

Matthew 3.11

"I baptize you with water for repentance, but he who is coming after me is mightier than I, whose sandals I am not worthy to carry. He will baptize you with the Holy Spirit and fire."

Theme

The Lord prepares the way for Messiah, the true seed of Abraham, to establish his Kingdom.

Setting

The Wilderness of Judea near the Jordan River

Major Characters

- John the Baptist
- Jewish People
- Pharisees and Sadducees – Jewish Religious Leaders

Plot

Introduction and Rising Action

1. John is a wild man who wears rough clothing and eats wild locusts and honey.
2. He preaches in the wilderness that the kingdom of God is at hand.
3. He calls for repentance ahead of the arrival of Messiah and baptizes many Jewish people in the Jordan River.

John the Baptist prepares the way for Messiah

Climax

4. The Pharisees and Sadducees are Jewish religious leaders who come to see what John is doing.

5. When he sees them, John calls them a brood of vipers.

6. He tells them that they must repent instead of relying on their ancestry for God's favor.

Falling Action and Resolution

7. John says that while he baptizes in water for repentance, Messiah will come and baptize with the Holy Spirit and with fire.

8. He warns the religious leaders that Messiah will bring the wrath of God against them if they do not repent.

Old Testament Foundation: The Principle of Reversal
(God has promised to raise up a leader to right the world)

Flee the Wrath to Come, Genesis 19 (p. 56)

The messenger is sent ahead to warn the people to flee the wrath to come.

Sodom and Gomorrah: a graphic example of human sinfulness and divine judgment. (See Isa. 3.9; 13.19; Jer. 23.14; Lam. 4.6; Ezek. 16.44-58; Amos 4.11; Matt. 10.15; 11.23-24; Luke 10.12; 17.28-30; 2 Pet. 2.6-9; Jude 7.)

Peter also makes clear that God's rescue of Lot prefigures his preservation and rescue of a remnant of humanity by grace from the coming judgment of sin and evil (2 Pet. 2.9).

Whose Side Are You On? Joshua 5.13-15

As the Lord required repentance and righteousness of his people to fight for them in the time of Joshua, so he calls his people through John to repent so that at the arrival of Messiah he could fight for them, not against them.

Christmas

··

The Birth of Christ

*Christmas celebrates the birth of Messiah, Jesus,
who is the incarnation of the Son of God, Mary's child.
He is the Word made flesh, the conqueror who enters this fallen world
to reveal to us the Father's love, to destroy the devil's work,
and to redeem his people from their sins.*

45 Journey to Bethlehem
Luke 2.1-5

Key Verse

Luke 2.4

And Joseph also went up from Galilee, from the town of Nazareth, to Judea, to the city of David, which is called Bethlehem, because he was of the house and lineage of David.

Theme 》

Jesus is the promised Messiah, the son of David, the new king of God's Kingdom.

Mary and Joseph journey to Bethlehem

Setting | The road from Nazareth to Bethlehem

Major Characters
- Joseph
- Mary

Plot

Introduction and Rising Action

1. The Roman Emperor Augustus calls for a census.
2. Everyone had to return to their hometown to be registered.

Climax

3. Joseph must return to Bethlehem, his hometown, because he of the house and family of David.
4. Mary, his betrothed, is pregnant with Jesus.
5. They make the journey together. It is likely that they traveled by donkey.

Falling Action and Resolution

6. The stage for the arrival of the Lord's Messiah is set.
7. Mary and Joseph are making the final leg of the journey of hope and anticipation that began all the way back in the Garden of Eden.

Old Testament Foundation: The Deliverer Is Born

The Lord Spoke through the Prophets, Micah 5.2 (p. 126)

All of the prophets anticipate the arrival of the Lord's Messiah. Micah foretold that Messiah would be born in Bethlehem.

The Birth of Jesus
Matthew 1.18-25; Luke 2.6-7

Key Verse

Luke 2.7

And she gave birth to her firstborn son and wrapped him in swaddling cloths and laid him in a manger, because there was no place for them in the inn.

Christ is born in Bethlehem!

Theme | Jesus is the Christ, the Son of God, born of a virgin.

Setting
- Nazareth – the town where Joseph and Mary live
- Bethlehem – where Jesus is born

Major Characters
- Joseph
- Mary
- The Angel of the Lord
- Jesus

Plot

Introduction and Rising Action

1. Mary is pregnant, and Joseph knows that he is not the father.
2. Joseph plans to call off their engagement and divorce her quietly.

Climax

3. The angel of the Lord appears to Joseph in a dream and tells him to take Mary as his wife.
4. The angel confirms that the child in Mary's womb was conceived by the Holy Spirit.

Falling Action and Resolution

5. Joseph takes Mary as his wife.
6. Mary gives birth to Jesus in a stable in Bethlehem lays him in a manger, because there is no room for them in the inn.

The Announcement of Christ's Birth to the Shepherds
Luke 2.8-20

Key Verse

Luke 2.14

"Glory to God in the highest, and on earth peace among those with whom he is pleased!"

The angels announce the birth of Jesus to the shepherds

Theme

The arrival of Christ the Lord is good news of great joy for all people!

Setting

The fields around Bethlehem

Major Characters

- Shepherds – keeping watch over their flocks
- The Angel of the Lord
- Mary and Joseph
- Jesus

Plot

Introduction and Rising Action

1. Around Bethlehem many shepherd are keeping watch over their flocks by night.
2. Suddenly, the Angel of the Lord appears to them with a great multitude of other angels.
3. He tells them to go find the Messiah (or Christ), who has been born this very night in Bethlehem.

Climax

4. The shepherds hurry to Bethlehem.
5. They find Mary and Joseph, and Jesus the newborn Lord, wrapped swaddling clothes, and lying in a manger.
6. The shepherds tell Mary and Joseph about the announcement of the angels.

Falling Action and Resolution

7. Everyone is amazed by what the shepherds say.
8. Mary treasures up the words in her heart.
9. The shepherds return to their flocks praising the Lord.

48 The Presentation of the Lord in the Temple
Luke 2.22-39

Key Verse

Luke 2.29-32

"Lord, now you are letting your servant depart in peace, according to your word; for my eyes have seen your salvation that you have prepared in the presence of all peoples, a light for revelation to the Gentiles, and for glory to your people Israel."

Luke 2.38

And coming up at that very hour she began to give thanks to God and to speak of him to all who were waiting for the redemption of Jerusalem.

Theme

Christ is the fulfillment of the Lord's promise of salvation for the world.

Simeon takes Jesus in his arms and praises God

Setting The Temple in Jerusalem

Major Characters

- Simeon
- Anna
- Mary and Joseph
- Jesus

The prophetess Anna praises God and tells others about Jesus

Plot

Introduction and Rising Action

1. Eight days after his birth, Mary and Joseph bring Jesus to the temple according to the requirements of Old Testament Law.

Climax

2. The Holy Spirit leads Simeon, a righteous and holy man, into the temple at this same time.

3. He takes Jesus in his arms and praises God for allowing him to see the Messiah. He then speaks a prophecy to Mary that Jesus, as Messiah, is destined for opposition and that her own soul would be pierced.

4. Anna, a prophet of the Lord, is also there and she begins to tell everyone around about Jesus.

Falling Action and Resolution

5. Mary and Joseph return home where Jesus grows strong and wise with the favor of God upon him.

Old Testament Foundation: The Deliverer Is Recognized

The Lord Gives the Law, Exodus 34.29-35

In his arrival, Messiah comes not to abolish the Law, but to fulfill it.

Epiphany

. . . .

The Manifestation of Christ

Epiphany commemorates the coming of the Magi,
the wise men from the East who followed the star in search of the Christ child.
This season emphasizes Christ's mission to and for the world.
The light of God's salvation is revealed to all peoples
in the person of Jesus, the Son of God.

The Adoration of the Magi
Matthew 2.1-12

Key Verse

Matthew 2.11

And going into the house, they saw the child with Mary his mother, and they fell down and worshiped him. Then, opening their treasures, they offered him gifts, gold and frankincense and myrrh.

The Magi give gifts to Jesus

Theme All nations will come to the light of Christ, the king of the Jews.

Setting
- Jerusalem
- Bethlehem

Major Characters
- The Magi from the East
- King Herod
- Jesus
- Mary

Plot

Introduction and Rising Action

1. Magi (wise men) from the East arrive in Jerusalem seeking the newborn king of the Jews. They observed his star rising and came to worship him.
2. King Herod is greatly troubled by the news and calls a secret meeting with the Magi.
3. He sends them on to Bethlehem but asks them to report back to him on where they find the child.

Climax

4. The Magi go to Bethlehem and the star they are following leads them directly to the house where Mary and Jesus are.
5. They kneel before Jesus and give him gifts of gold, frankincense, and myrrh.

Falling Action and Resolution

6. The Magi are warned in a dream not to return to Herod, so they leave Bethlehem return to their homeland without going back through Jerusalem.

The Baptism of the Lord
Matthew 3.13-17

Key Verse   Matthew 3.16-17

And when Jesus was baptized, immediately he went up from the water, and behold, the heavens were opened to him, and he saw the Spirit of God descending like a dove and coming to rest on him; and behold, a voice from heaven said, "This is my beloved Son, with whom I am well pleased."

Theme   Christ is the beloved Son of God the Father.

Setting   The Jordan River

John baptizes Jesus in the Jordan River

Major Characters

- John the Baptist
- Jesus
- God the Father

Plot

Introduction and Rising Action

1. Jesus comes down to the Jordan river to be baptized by John.

Climax

2. John objects saying the he needs to be baptized by Jesus.
3. Jesus convinces to baptize him by saying that it is necessary to fulfill all righteousness.
4. As Jesus comes up from the water the Spirit of God descends like a dove and rests on him.

Falling Action and Resolution

5. The voice of the Father comes from heaven and declares Jesus as his Son and beloved.

Old Testament Foundation: Fully Human/Fully Divine

Noah's Ark, Genesis 6-9 (p. 46)

As the Lord rescued Noah and his family through the waters, so too Christ enters the waters in order to fulfill all righteousness and bring about a a great rescue from the coming destruction.

The Red Sea, Exodus 14-15 (p. 70)

As Moses and the people passed through the Red Sea and then were led up into the wilderness to be tested, so too Christ passes through the waters and is led into the wilderness.

The Temptation of Our Lord
Matthew 4.1-11

Key Verse

Matthew 4.4

But he answered, "It is written, 'Man shall not live by bread alone, but by every word that comes from the mouth of God.'"

Theme

Christ came to destroy the works of the devil and deliver humanity from his power.

Setting

The wilderness

Major Characters

- The Holy Spirit
- Jesus
- Satan – the tempter

Plot

Introduction and Rising Action

1. The Holy Spirit leads Jesus into the wilderness to be tempted by the devil.
2. Jesus fasts for forty days and nights.

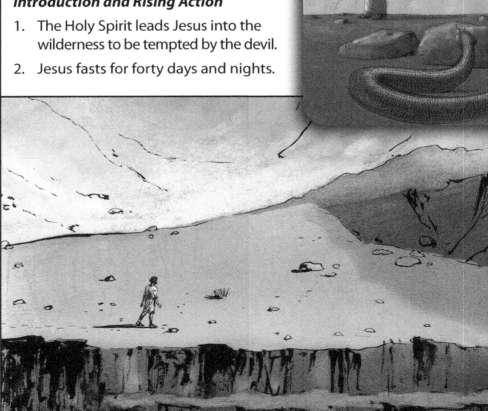

Jesus being tempted by the devil in the wilderness

Climax

3. The tempter comes to Jesus and gives him three temptations. Each time Jesus responds with Scripture.

4. He tempts Jesus to turn stones into bread. Jesus responds that he lives not by bread alone, but by the Word of God.

5. Satan tempts Jesus to throw himself off the pinnacle of the temple to see if the angels will catch him. Jesus refuses to put God to the test.

6. Satan then takes Jesus to high mountain and tempts him with authority over all the nations of the world, if only Jesus will worship him. Jesus responds that he will worship and serve only the Lord.

Falling Action and Resolution

7. The devil leaves Jesus and the angels attend to him.

Old Testament Foundation: Recapitulation
(He's the new David, Prophet, Israel, "every failure taken up and corrected" substitutionary atonement his life substituted for all of humanity)

The Serpent in Eden, Genesis 3.1-7 (p. 38)

Where Adam and Eve fell to the temptation of Satan, Christ resists and overcomes temptation.

The Israelites in the Wilderness, Numbers 14.11-45 (p. 78)

As Israel faced temptations in the wilderness, so Christ is led into the wilderness to be tempted.

The Calling of the Disciples
Matthew 4.18-22

Key Verse

Matthew 4.19

And he said to them, "Follow me, and I will make you fishers of men."

Theme

Christ calls disciples who will gather his people into his kingdom.

Setting

The Sea of Galilee

Jesus calls his first disciples

Major Characters

- Jesus
- Simon (Peter) and Andrew – brothers, fishermen
- James and John – brothers, fishermen
- Zebedee – father of James and John

Plot

Introduction and Rising Action

1. Simon and Andrew are fishing on the Sea of Galilee.

Climax

2. Jesus is walking and calls the brothers to follow him as his disciples.
3. He promises that from now on, they will fish for people.
4. Immediately, they leave their work and follow Jesus.

Falling Action and Resolution

5. The scene repeats with brothers James and John.
6. They are mending nets with their father Zebedee when Jesus calls them.
7. Immediately, they leave their father and their work to follow Jesus.

Old Testament Foundation: God's Reign and the End of the Curse

The Promise to Abraham, Genesis 12.15 (p. 52)

The promise that God made to Abraham to make his descendants as numerous as the stars he is fulfilling in Christ who calls all people to become children of Abraham by faith.

53 | The Feeding of the Five Thousand
John 6.1-15

Key Verse

John 6.11

Jesus then took the loaves, and when he had given thanks, he distributed them to those who were seated. So also the fish, as much as they wanted.

Theme »

Christ is the true bread of heaven.

Setting 📍

The eastern side of the Sea of Galilee

Jesus feeds 5,000 with a little boy's lunch

Major Characters

- Jesus
- Jesus's disciples
- A large crowd of about 5,000.

Plot

Introduction and Rising Action

1. Because of the miracles he is performing, a large crowd of about 5,000 people follow Jesus east of the Sea of Galilee.
2. Jesus asks his disciple Philip how they are going to get food for the crowd.
3. Philip replies that six months' wages would not buy enough food for them.

Climax

4. Andrew finds a young boy who has five loaves of bread and two fish.
5. Jesus takes the small meal, gives thanks to God, and begins to distribute the bread and fish to all those around.
6. Everyone is able to eat as much as they want.

Falling Action and Resolution

7. When everyone is full, the disciples pick up twelve baskets full of leftover fragments.
8. The people proclaim that Jesus is the Lord's prophet.

The Gerasene Demoniac
Mark 5.1-20

Key Verse

Mark 5.19

And he did not permit him but said to him, "Go home to your friends and tell them how much the Lord has done for you, and how he has had mercy on you."

Theme

Christ came to destroy the works of the devil and deliver humanity from his power.

Setting

The country of the Gerasenes
(East side of the Sea of Galilee)

Jesus heals the Gerasene demoniac

Major Characters

- Jesus
- The disciples
- Unnamed demoniac
- A legion of demons
- The townspeople

Plot

Introduction and Rising Action

1. Jesus crosses the Sea of Galilee by boat.
2. As soon as Jesus steps ashore, a demoniac who lives in the tombs begins to run toward him and shout at him.
3. The demoniac lives among the tombs howling and hurting himself, and no one can control him.

Climax

4. The demoniac asks Jesus not to torment him.
5. When Jesus asks his name, he responds that there is a legion of demons in the man.
6. The demons ask to be sent into a herd of pigs on the hillside. Jesus grants this request, and the pigs rush off the hill and drown themselves in the sea.

Falling Action and Resolution

7. The pig herders run off to get the townspeople.
8. When the townspeople arrive, they ask Jesus to leave their region.
9. The man who had the legion of demons begs to follow Jesus. Jesus tells him to go tell everyone what the Lord has done for him.
10. The man amazes everyone with his story.

Jairus's Daughter
Mark 5.21-24, 35-43

Key Verse

Mark 5.36

But overhearing what they said, Jesus said to the ruler of the synagogue, "Do not fear, only believe."

Theme

Christ overcomes the curse and conquers death itself.

Setting

A town on the Sea of Galilee

Jesus heals Jairus's daughter

Major Characters

- Jesus
- Jairus – a synagogue leader
- Jairus's daughter
- A crowd of mourners

Plot

Introduction and Rising Action

1. Jairus, a synagogue leader, approaches Jesus because his daughter is on the verge of death.

2. Jesus goes with Jairus to the girl, but he gets delayed. Before Jesus arrives, someone comes from Jairus's house and announces that the girl has died.

Climax

3. They arrive at Jairus's house to find a large crowd of mourners weeping and wailing.

4. The crowd laughs at Jesus when he says the girl is merely asleep.

5. Jesus takes only a few people into the room. He tells the little girl to get up.

Falling Action and Resolution

6. Immediately, the girl gets up and walks around the house.

7. Everyone is amazed at Jesus, but he orders them to tell no one about this.

56 The Hemorrhaging Woman
Mark 5.25-34

Key Verse

Mark 5.34

And he said to her, "Daughter, your faith has made you well; go in peace, and be healed of your disease."

Theme

Christ brings the healing and wholeness of God's Kingdom.

Setting

On the road to Jairus's house

A woman healed after twelve years of hemorrhaging

Major Characters

- Jesus
- An unnamed woman who has been hemorrhaging for twelve years
- A large crowd
- The disciples

Plot

Introduction and Rising Action

1. A woman who has suffered with hemorrhaging for twelve years seeks out Jesus.
2. She has spent everything on doctors but has not gotten any better.
3. She believes that if she can touch Jesus's cloak she will be healed.

Climax

4. She makes her way through the crowd. As soon as she touches Jesus's cloak, the blood dries up.
5. As Jesus is journeying to heal Jairus's daughter, he stops and look around. He asks who touched him.
6. The disciples are shocked that Jesus asks this in a large crowd. Jesus felt that power has gone out from him.

Falling Action and Resolution

7. The woman comes before Jesus and tells him the truth.
8. Jesus tells her that she can go in peace, and that her faith has healed her.

The Parable of the Sower and the Soils
Matthew 13.1-8, 18-23

Key Verse

Matthew 13.23

As for what was sown on good soil, this is the one who hears the word and understands it. He indeed bears fruit and yields, in one case a hundredfold, in another sixty, and in another thirty.

Theme

The good news of Christ and his Kingdom is only fruitful in some who hear it.

The parable of the sower and the soils

Setting | Beside the sea

Major Characters

- Jesus – the storyteller
- A crowd of people
- The disciples
- The sower
- The evil one

Plot

Introduction and Rising Action

1. Jesus tells a story to a crowd of people while he sits by the sea.
2. Later, when they are alone, the disciples ask him to explain the parable.

Climax (The Parable and Its Meaning)

3. A Sower goes to sow some seed. This seed is the word of the kingdom.
4. Some seed falls by the path and is eaten by the birds. This represents one who hears the word, but the evil one comes and snatches it away.
5. Some seed falls into rocky soil where is sprouts quickly but dies. This represents one who hears and receives the word, but who quickly falls away because of difficulties.
6. Some seed falls among thorns and is choked. This represents those who hears the word and receive it, but the world chokes out any fruitfulness.
7. Some seed falls on fertile soil and yield a crop of thirty, sixty or a hundredfold. This represents those who hear the word and receive it, and who bears the fruit of the Kingdom.

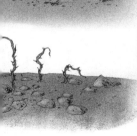

Falling Action and Resolution

8. Jesus concludes his parable saying "He who has ears, let him hear."

58

The Mustard Seed

Matthew 13.31-32

Key Verse

Matthew 13.31

He put another parable before them, saying, "The kingdom of heaven is like a grain of mustard seed that a man took and sowed in his field."

Theme

Starting with a few disciples, Christ's Kingdom will grow to encompass all nations and all creation.

Jesus compares the Kingdom of God to a mustard bush

Setting Beside the sea

Major Characters
- Jesus – the storyteller
- A sower

Plot

Introduction and Rising Action

1. Jesus is giving parables and images to describe God's Kingdom.

Climax (The Parable)

2. He says the Kingdom of heaven is like a mustard seed that a sower sows in his field.
3. It begins as the tiniest of seed.
4. However, when it is fully grown it is the largest of shrubs and becomes a tree.

Falling Action and Resolution

5. All the birds of the air can come and make their nests in the branches of this great tree.

59

Jesus Walks on the Water
Matthew 14.22-33

Key Verse

Matthew 14.33

And those in the boat worshiped him, saying, "Truly you are the Son of God."

Theme

Christ is the Son of God, the Lord of all creation.

Jesus walks on the water

Setting
- A lonely mountain
- The Sea of Galilee

Major Characters
- Jesus
- The disciples
- Peter

Plot

Introduction and Rising Action

1. After dismissing the crowds and sending his disciples ahead in a boat, Jesus goes up on a mountain by himself to pray.
2. The boat is battered by winds and waves, and drifts far away from the shore.

Climax

3. Jesus comes to them walking on the water.
4. The disciples are terrified that it is a ghost until Jesus calls out to them and calms them.
5. Peter gets out of the boat and begins to walk toward Jesus on the water. He begins to sink when he looks around and sees the wind whipping up.
6. Jesus catches him by the arm and saves him from sinking.

Falling Action and Resolution

7. Jesus asks Peter why he doubted.
8. When they get back in the boat, the disciples worship him saying that he truly is the Son of God.

The Transfiguration
Matthew 17.1-8

Key Verse

Matthew 17.5

He was still speaking when, behold, a bright cloud overshadowed them, and a voice from the cloud said, "This is my beloved Son, with whom I am well pleased; listen to him."

Theme

Christ is the Son who shines the Father's glory and truth into the world.

The Transfiguration of Christ

Setting | A high mountain

Major Characters |
- Jesus
- Peter, James, and John – Jesus's inner circle of disciples
- Moses and Elijah
- God the Father

Plot

Introduction and Rising Action

1. Jesus takes Peter, James, and John up a high mountain to be alone.
2. When they get up there, Jesus's face and clothes are transfigured and begin to shine brightly.

Climax

3. Moses and Elijah appear with Jesus, speaking with him.
4. Peter suggests that they build three tents on the mountain.
5. As he is saying this, a bright cloud envelops them and the voice of the Father tells them to listen to Jesus, his beloved Son.

Falling Action and Resolution

6. The disciples fall on their faces terrified.
7. When they look up again, they see only Jesus standing there.

Old Testament Foundation: The Messiah as Prophet and Law Giver

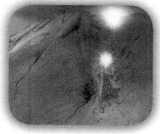

Moses's Shining Face, Exodus 34.29

As Moses's face shone when he had been on the mountain with the Lord, so Jesus's face shines on the mountain of transfiguration.

Lent

. . . .

The Lowliness of Christ

*The Lenten Season, a forty-day period
starting on Ash Wednesday and ending on Holy Saturday of Holy Week,
calls us to reflect on Jesus's suffering, crucifixion, and death.
As disciples of the humble Nazarene, we embrace his lowliness and humility,
seeking to share the mind of him who was obedient to death,
even death on a cross.*

The Great Confession
Mark 8.27-9.1

Key Verse

Mark 8.34

And calling the crowd to him with his disciples, he said to them, "If anyone would come after me, let him deny himself and take up his cross and follow me.

Theme

Jesus, the Messiah, will establish his Kingdom by suffering, dying, and rising again.

"Get behind me, Satan!"

Setting The villages around Caesarea Philippi

Major Characters

- Jesus
- Peter
- The other disciples

Plot

Introduction and Rising Action

1. Jesus asks his disciples who people are saying that he is.
2. They say that the crowds think he is either John the Baptist or Elijah.
3. He then asks who they (his disciples) say he is.
4. Peter speaks for the group and declares, "You are the Christ."
5. He begins to teach them that the Christ came to suffer, to die, and to rise again.

Climax

6. Peter rebukes Jesus for saying this.
7. Jesus in turn rebukes Peter, saying, "Get behind me, Satan."

Falling Action and Resolution

8. Jesus explains that his followers must deny themselves, take up their cross, and follow him.
9. He declares that his followers must be willing to lose their lives for his sake.

62 The Good Samaritan
Luke 10.25-37

Key Verse

Luke 10.29

But he, desiring to justify himself, said to Jesus, "And who is my neighbor?"

Luke 10.36-37

"Which of these three, do you think, proved to be a neighbor to the man who fell among the robbers?" He said, "The one who showed him mercy." And Jesus said to him, "You go, and do likewise."

Jesus tells a parable of a man who is beaten and left for dead

A Levite avoids the man

The Samaritan helps the man

Theme Christ's Kingdom demands that we love our neighbors as ourselves.

Setting Jesus is telling a parable to a self-righteous lawyer

Major Characters

- Jesus
- A lawyer – an expert in the Law of Moses
- A man beaten and left for dead
- A priest
- A Levite
- A Samaritan

Plot

Introduction and Rising Action

1. A lawyer who wants to justify himself, ask Jesus what he must do to fulfill the command to love his neighbor and inherit eternal life.
2. In response, Jesus tells him a parable.

Climax (The Parable)

3. A man is traveling to Jerusalem when he is robbed, beaten, and left for dead.
4. Both a priest and Levite pass by and do not help the man.
5. A despised Samaritan passes by and helps the man. He bandages his wounds, brings him to an inn, and pays for the man to stay while he heals.

 Falling Action and Resolution

6. Jesus asks the lawyer who fulfilled the commandment to love one's neighbor.
7. When the lawyer indicates that it is the Samaritan, Jesus commands him to go and do likewise.

The Lost Sheep
Luke 15.1-7

Key Verse

Luke 15.7

Just so, I tell you, there will be more joy in heaven over one sinner who repents than over ninety-nine righteous persons who need no repentance.

The shepherd leaves the ninety-nine to find the one lost sheep

Theme Christ came to seek and save what was lost.

Setting The Pharisees are upset that Jesus welcomes tax collectors and sinners.

Major Characters

- Jesus – the storyteller
- A shepherd
- The sheep

Plot

Introduction and Rising Action

1. Jesus tells a parable to a group of Pharisees who are grumbling that he welcomes tax collectors and sinners.

Climax (The Parable)

2. A shepherd has a flock of one hundred sheep.
3. One sheep wanders away into the wilderness, but ninety-nine stay together.
4. The shepherd leaves the ninety-nine to seek and save the one lost sheep.
5. When he finds the sheep, he calls together his friends and neighbors to celebrate that he has found his lost sheep.

Falling Action and Resolution

6. Jesus explains that all heaven rejoices greatly over one sinner who repents.

64 The Prodigal Son
Luke 15.11-32

Key Verse

Luke 15.13

Not many days later, the younger son gathered all he had and took a journey into a far country, and there he squandered his property in reckless living.

Luke 15.23-24

And bring the fattened calf and kill it, and let us eat and celebrate. For this my son was dead, and is alive again; he was lost, and is found.' And they began to celebrate.

The parable of the prodigal son; the son leaves the father

Theme The Lord and his Kingdom celebrate when the lost come home to him.

Setting The Pharisees are upset that Jesus welcomes tax collectors and sinners.

Major Characters
- Jesus – the storyteller
- The father
- The younger son
- The older brother

Plot

The son returns

Introduction and Rising Action

1. Jesus is telling a story.
2. A father has two sons. The younger son demands his share of the inheritance.
3. He goes into a far country and wastes all his money on wild living.

Climax

4. The younger son reaches a low point when he is so hungry that he longs to eat pig slop. He decides to return to his father's house as a servant.
5. When he arrives home, the father is so glad to see him that the runs to greet him, clothes him the best clothes, and throws a great feast of celebration.
6. The older brother refuses to come to the feast, so the father goes to speak with him. The older brother is angry about the father celebrating the return of the younger son.

Falling Action and Resolution

7. The father explains that he has to celebrate because the younger son was dead and has come to life, that he was lost and has been found.

Zaccheus
Luke 19.1-10

Key Verse

Luke 19.9-10

And Jesus said to him, "Today salvation has come to this house, since he also is a son of Abraham. For the Son of Man came to seek and to save the lost."

Jesus calls to
Zaccheus

Theme | Christ came to seek and save the lost.

Setting

- A road through Jericho
- Zacchaeus's house

Major Characters

- Zacchaeus
- Jesus
- A crowd of people

Plot

Introduction and Rising Action

1. Jesus is passing through Jericho.
2. Zacchaeus is a rich tax collector who is desperate to see Jesus.
3. He is a short man, so he climbs a sycamore tree to see Jesus over the large crowd.

Climax

4. Jesus stops and looks up at Zacchaeus. He tells Zacchaeus to come down from the tree so they can go to his house.
5. Many in the crowd grumble about this because Zacchaeus is a sinner.
6. Zacchaeus announces that he will give half his possessions to the poor and restore four-fold anything he has stolen.

Falling Action and Resolution

7. Jesus proclaims that salvation has come to Zacchaeus's house this day.
8. He says that seeking and saving the lost sinners like Zacchaeus is the reason he has come.

66 Jesus Journeys to Jerusalem
Mark 10.32-45

Key Verse

Mark 10.45

"For even the Son of Man came not to be served but to serve, and to give his life as a ransom for many."

Theme

True greatness in Christ's Kingdom means becoming a servant.

Jesus on the road going up to Jerusalem

Setting On the road from Judea beyond the Jordan up to Jerusalem

Major Characters
- Jesus
- James and John
- The other disciples

Plot

Introduction and Rising Action

1. The disciples are amazed and afraid as Jesus resolutely walks toward Jerusalem.
2. Jesus once again explains to them that he will be arrested, beaten, and killed in Jerusalem, but that he will rise again.

Climax

3. Two of Jesus's disciples, James and John, approach Jesus and ask to sit at his right and left hand in his Kingdom.
4. Jesus explains that these positions are not his to grant.
5. The other disciples get angry with James and John for requesting this honor.

Falling Action and Resolution

6. Jesus explains that true greatness in his Kingdom is not a matter of high position.
7. Whoever wants to be great in the Kingdom of Christ must become a servant of all.
8. Even the Christ, God's Messiah, came to serve and to give his life as a ransom for many.

Holy Week

· ·

The Passion of Christ

Holy Week recalls the events of our Lord's suffering and death.
We recall his triumphant entry into Jerusalem on Palm Sunday,
his giving of the commandments on Maundy Thursday,
his crucifixion and burial on Good Friday,
and the solemn vigil of Saturday night before Easter Sunday.

67

The Triumphal Entry
Matthew 21.1-11

Key Verse

Matthew 21.9

And the crowds that went before him and that followed him were shouting, "Hosanna to the Son of David! Blessed is he who comes in the name of the Lord! Hosanna in the highest!"

Theme

Christ is the Lord's king come to save God's people.

Jesus enters Jerusalem on a donkey

Setting The road from the Mount of Olives into Jerusalem

Major Characters
- Jesus
- The disciples
- A large crowd

Plot

Introduction and Rising Action

1. Jesus sends two disciples to retrieve a donkey and her colt for him to ride.
2. He tells them that if anyone asks why they are taking the animals to say, "The Lord needs them."

Climax

3. Jesus rides the donkey from the Mount of Olives into Jerusalem.
4. As he rides a great crowd gathers and spreads their cloaks on the road. They cut palm branches and wave them in celebration.
5. Everyone is shouting, "Hosanna to the Son of David!"

Falling Action and Resolution

6. The whole city is stirred up by the news that the prophet from Nazareth has arrived in Jerusalem.

 Old Testament Foundation: The City of the Great King

The Lord Spoke through the Prophets, Zechariah 9.9 (p. 126)

The Messiah is revealed to the people of God.

The Last Supper
Luke 22.7-23

Key Verse

Luke 22.19-20

And he took bread, and when he had given thanks, he broke it and gave it to them, saying, "This is my body, which is given for you. Do this in remembrance of me." And likewise the cup after they had eaten, saying, "This cup that is poured out for you is the new covenant in my blood."

Theme

Christ offers the sacrifice of his own body and blood for his followers to remember and reenact his mighty saving deeds.

Setting

An upper room in a house in or around Jerusalem

Major Characters

- Jesus
- Peter and John
- The disciples

Jesus shares a final Passover meal with the disciples

Plot ### Introduction and Rising Action

1. When it comes time to celebrate the Passover, Jesus sends Peter and John to find a man carrying a water jar, who will lead them to the place.

2. They go and find it just as Jesus has said and prepare the Passover meal.

 ### Climax

3. During the meal Jesus takes bread, and when he had given thanks, he broke it and gave it to them, saying, "This is my body, which is given for you. Do this in remembrance of me."

4. After they had eaten he took the cup saying, "This cup that is poured out for you is the new covenant in my blood."

Falling Action and Resolution

5. Jesus tells the disciples that one of them will betray him.

6. They are disturbed by this news and try to figure out which one of them would do such a thing.

69 Jesus Washes the Disciples' Feet
John 13.1-20

Key Verse

John 13.14-15

If I then, your Lord and Teacher, have washed your feet, you also ought to wash one another's feet. For I have given you an example, that you also should do just as I have done to you.

Jesus washes the disciples' feet

Theme Christ cleanses his people from sin by the offering of himself as a suffering servant.

Setting An upper room in a house in or around Jerusalem

Major Characters
- Jesus
- Judas
- Peter
- The disciples

Plot

Introduction and Rising Action

1. Jesus knows that his hour has come, that Judas is ready to betray him, and that he was about to depart.
2. At supper, he stood up and stripped to his undergarments.
3. He then proceeds to do the menial task of washing the feet of the disciples.

Climax

4. When Jesus comes to him, Peter tries to refuse to let the Lord wash his feet.
5. Jesus tells him that if he will not allow his feet to be washed, Peter has no share with Christ.
6. Peter then exclaims that he wants the Lord to bathe his whole body!

Falling Action and Resolution

7. Jesus explains that he is already clean, and only needs his feet washed.
8. However, he tells the disciples that not all of them are clean. He knew what Judas was about to do.

The Passion: Prayer in the Garden
Matthew 26.36-46

Key Verse

Matthew 26.39

And going a little farther he fell on his face and prayed, saying, "My Father, if it be possible, let this cup pass from me; nevertheless, not as I will, but as you will."

Theme

Christ submits completely to the will of the Father and his kingdom purposes.

Setting

The Garden of Gethsemane

Major Characters

- Jesus
- Peter, James, and John

Plot

Introduction and Rising Action

1. Late at night, Jesus took his disciples to Gethsemane to pray.
2. He took Peter, James, and John with him and asks them to stay awake with him while he prays.

Climax

3. He goes off alone, falls on his face, and cries out to the Father to let the cup of suffering pass from him.
4. Jesus, however, submits to the will of the Father saying, "Not as I will, but as you will."
5. When he returned to the disciples they were sleeping. He urges them again to stay awake.
6. He returns and prays in the same way two more times.

Falling Action and Resolution

7. When he finishes, he rouses the disciples. His betrayer is arriving at Gethsemane as he speaks.

Jesus prays in the Garden of Gethsemane

Old Testament Foundation: Types of Christ

Joseph: A Picture of Christ, Genesis 37-45 (p. 60)

- *The beloved of his father who was sent to his kinsman.*

- *Hated by his brothers, who plotted together to kill him.*

- *Rejected by his brothers the first time and considered dead.*

- *Sold for "blood money" (pieces of silver).*

- *Imprisoned with two criminals, one who "died" and the other who "lived."*

- *Raised and exalted to a place of authority and power next to the king.*

- *Gives all honor to the king and delivers all glory and treasure into the king's hands.*

- *Brings his people to repentance and self-knowledge.*

- *He is acknowledged to be the savior of his people and their ruler.*

Betrayal in the Garden
Matthew 26.47-56

Key Verse   Matthew 26.53-54

"Do you think that I cannot appeal to my Father, and he will at once send me more than twelve legions of angels? But how then should the Scriptures be fulfilled, that it must be so?"

Theme   Christ submits completely to the will of the Father and his kingdom purposes.

Setting   The Garden of Gethsemane

Major Characters

- Jesus
- Judas
- An armed crowd from the priests and elders
- Peter – the disciple with a sword

Judas betrays Jesus with a kiss

Plot | ### Introduction and Rising Action

1. Judas has betrayed Jesus to the Jewish priests and elders.

2. They give him an armed crowd to go detain Jesus. Judas arranges that he will kiss Jesus to identify him for the crowd.

 ### Climax

3. When Judas arrives at Gethsemane, he greets Jesus with a kiss.

4. The armed crowd with Judas seizes Jesus.

5. One of Jesus's disciples (Peter) tries to defend Jesus by cutting off the ear of one of the crowd.

6. Jesus rebukes Peter, telling him that this must take place to fulfill the Scriptures.

Falling Action and Resolution

7. The disciples flee as Jesus is taken away.

The Trial before Pilate
John 18.28-19.16

Key Verse

John 18.38

Pilate said to him, "What is truth?" After he had said this, he went back outside to the Jews and told them, "I find no guilt in him."

Theme

Christ offers himself as a spotless substitute to be sacrificed for sin.

Setting

The governor's headquarters

The Jews convince Pilate to have Jesus killed

Major Characters

- Jesus
- Pilate – the Roman governor
- Roman soldiers
- The Jewish religious leaders

Plot

Introduction and Rising Action

1. After questioning Jesus, the Jewish religious leaders take Jesus to Pilate, the Roman governor.
2. They request that Jesus be put to death.

Climax

3. Pilate questions Jesus but finds no guilt in him worthy of death.
4. He tries to free Jesus as the customary Passover prisoner release, but the leaders choose Barabbas instead.
5. Pilate has Jesus flogged and mocked. Again he present Jesus to the people seeking to release Jesus.

Falling Action and Resolution

6. The people reject Jesus as their king and refuse to allow his release.
7. Pilate hands Jesus over to be crucified.

Pilate has Jesus flogged

The Crucifixion: Jesus Carries His Cross
John 19.16-30

Key Verse

John 19.18

There they crucified him, and with him two others, one on either side, and Jesus between them.

Theme ≫

Christ offers himself as a spotless substitute to be sacrificed, bearing our sins in his body on the cross.

Setting

Golgotha – The Place of the Skull

Jesus carries his cross to Golgotha

Major Characters

- Jesus
- Pilate
- Roman soldiers
- John
- Mary and two other women

Plot

Introduction and Rising Action

1. Jesus carries his cross to Golgotha, where he will be crucified.
2. Pilate writes an inscription to put on the cross, "Jesus of Nazareth, King of the Jews."

Climax

3. The Roman soldiers crucify Jesus
4. In fulfillment of Scripture, they gamble over his tunic.
5. From the cross, Jesus appoints John to care for his mother, Mary.

Falling Action and Resolution

6. After receiving a drink of sour wine, Jesus declares, "It is finished," and he dies.

Old Testament Foundation: Jesus's Death Foreshadowed

The Scapegoat, Leviticus 16.20-21

As all the sin of Israel is laid on the scapegoat, so all of our iniquities are laid on Christ.

Abraham Sacrificing Isaac, Genesis 22.1-19 (p. 58)

The Lord stayed Abraham's hand before he killed his beloved son, Isaac, and provided a ram as a substitute. God the Father put forward his own beloved Son as our substitute and stayed the hand of his own wrath against human sin.

The Crucifixion: Jesus and the Two Criminals
Luke 23.32-43

Key Verse

Luke 23.42-43

And he said, "Jesus, remember me when you come into your kingdom." And he said to him, "Truly, I say to you, today you will be with me in paradise."

Theme

Christ offers himself as a spotless substitute to be sacrificed so we can be forgiven.

Setting

Golgotha, while Jesus is hanging on the cross

Major Characters

- Jesus
- Two criminals crucified with him

Jesus is crucified between two criminals

Plot

Introduction and Rising Action

1. Jesus is crucified in the middle of two criminals.

2. He asks his Father to forgive the soldiers, because they do not understand what they are doing.

3. The soldiers continue to mock Jesus.

Climax

4. As he is suffering on the cross, one of the criminals begins to mock him as well.

5. The other criminal stops him saying that Jesus has done nothing wrong to deserve this punishment.

6. He asks Jesus to remember him when he comes into his Kingdom.

Falling Action and Resolution

7. Jesus tells the repentant criminal that today, he would be with him in paradise.

Old Testament Foundation: Pictures of Christ's Sacrifice

The Bronze Serpent, Numbers 21.4-9

As Moses lifted up the bronze serpent in the wilderness, so Jesus was lifted up on the cross for the healing of God's people.

The Lamb on the Altar, Deuteronomy 16.1-8

The Blood on the Doorposts, Exodus 12.7-13 (p. 68)

As the spotless lamb is slaughtered, and the children of Israel are saved by its blood, so too Christ our spotless Passover lamb has been slain and his blood redeems us from death.

The Crucifixion: The Onlookers
Matthew 27.45-56

Key Verse

Matthew 27.51

And behold, the curtain of the temple was torn in two, from top to bottom. And the earth shook, and the rocks were split.

Theme

Christ offers himself as a spotless substitute to be sacrificed for the reconciliation of all things to God.

Darkness covers the land and Jesus's followers look on from a distance

Setting
- Golgotha, while Jesus is hanging on the cross
- The Temple

Major Characters
- Jesus
- A centurion
- Women who had been following Jesus

Plot

Introduction and Rising Action

1. As Jesus hangs on the cross, darkness covers the land in the middle of the day.

Climax

2. Jesus cries out, "My God, my God, why have you forsaken me?"
3. He yields up his spirit to death.
4. As he dies, the curtain in the temple that sections off the Holy of Holies rips in two from the top.
5. There is a great earthquake and many dead saints are raised to life.
6. The centurion who was guarding the cross exclaims in amazement, "Truly this was the Son of God!"

Falling Action and Resolution

7. Many women who had followed Jesus also watched everything unfold from a distance.

The Burial of Jesus
John 19.38-42

Key Verse

John 19.38

After these things Joseph of Arimathea, who was a disciple of Jesus, but secretly for fear of the Jews, asked Pilate that he might take away the body of Jesus, and Pilate gave him permission. So he came and took away his body.

Joseph of Arimathea and Nicodemus prepare to put Jesus in a tomb

Theme Christ offers himself as a spotless substitute to be sacrificed and conquer death.

Setting A garden near Golgotha

Major Characters
- Joseph of Arimathea
- Pilate
- Nicodemus

Plot

Introduction and Rising Action

1. Joseph of Arimathea has been a secret disciple of Jesus out of fear of the Jewish leaders.
2. After the death of Jesus, Joseph of Arimathea asks for his body.

Climax

3. Pilate grants Joseph the body of Jesus.
4. Nicodemus and Joseph prepare Jesus's body for burial by wrapping him in linen cloth that is rubbed with myrrh and aloes.

Falling Action and Resolution

5. They place Jesus in an empty tomb in a garden near Golgoltha.

Eastertide

The Resurrection of Christ

On Easter Sunday we celebrate the bodily resurrection of Jesus.
The same lowly Nazarene – he who was betrayed by his own disciple,
who suffered under Pilate's cruel gaze, who was crucified
on a Roman cross, and who was buried in a borrowed tomb –
the same Lord rose triumphantly on the third day.
Jesus has risen from death to life through the power of God.
"Christ is risen! He is risen, indeed!"

The Guards at the Tomb
Matthew 27.62-66

Key Verse Matthew 27.65

So they went and made the tomb secure by sealing the stone and setting a guard.

Theme Christ has risen from the dead, victorious over the grave.

Setting
- Pilate's Headquarters
- The tomb of Jesus

Guarding Jesus's tomb

Major Characters

- The chief priests and Pharisees
- Pilate
- Guards

Plot

Introduction and Rising Action

1. The day after Jesus's crucifixion, the chief priests and Pharisees gather before Pilate.

Climax

2. They remind Pilate that Jesus had predicted that he would rise from the dead.

3. They ask Pilate to make the tomb secure so that Jesus's disciples cannot come steal the body and falsely claim that Jesus has risen from the dead.

Falling Action and Resolution

4. Pilate grants the request, and they make the tomb as secure as they can.

Old Testament Foundation: The Victory of God

The Captivity, 2 Chronicles 36.15-18 (p. 110)

As God's people are exiled as captive, so Christ is exiled to the captivity of the grave.

Jonah, Jonah 1-4 (p. 108)

As Jonah was in the belly of the whale three days and three nights, so Jesus rose on the third day.

The Guards at the Tomb: Part 2
Matthew 28.1-4

Key Verse

Matthew 28.2

And behold, there was a great earthquake, for an angel of the Lord descended from heaven and came and rolled back the stone and sat on it.

Terrified
guards flee
the tomb

Theme Christ has risen from the dead, victorious over death.

Setting The tomb of Jesus

Major Characters
- Mary Magdelene and another woman named Mary
- An angel of the Lord
- The guards at the tomb

Plot

Introduction and Rising Action

1. At dawn on the first day of the week, Mary Magdalene and another woman named Mary go to the tomb of Jesus.

Climax

2. There had been a great earthquake, and an angel of the Lord had from heaven.

3. The angel rolled away the stone that covered the entrance to the tomb and sat on it.

Falling Action and Resolution

4. The guards that had been stationed by the chief priests and Pharisees ran away and fainted in terror.

79

The Women at the Tomb
Luke 24.1-12

Key Verse

Luke 24.5-7

And as they were frightened and bowed their faces to the ground, the men said to them, "Why do you seek the living among the dead? He is not here, but has risen. Remember how he told you, while he was still in Galilee, that the Son of Man must be delivered into the hands of sinful men and be crucified and on the third day rise."

Three women come to Jesus's tomb and find it open and empty

Theme   Christ has risen from the dead and lives forevermore.

Setting   The tomb of Jesus

Major Characters
- Two men in dazzling clothing
- Three women who had followed Jesus
- Peter

Plot   **Introduction and Rising Action**

1. Three women who had watched where Jesus had been buried came to the tomb.
2. They were wondering how they were going to roll away the stone.

 Climax

3. When they arrive at the tomb they are shocked to find the stone rolled away, and the tomb empty.
4. In the confusion, two angelic men appear to them. They ask why the women are seeking Jesus among the dead.
5. Jesus is not in the tomb. He is risen, just as he promised!

Falling Action and Resolution

6. The women returned to the disciples to tell them what they had seen and heard.
7. Only Peter is willing to believe the women. He runs to the tomb and finds it empty, just as the women had said.

80

Jesus Appears to Mary
John 20.11-18

Key Verse

John 20.16

Jesus said to her, "Mary." She turned and said to him in Aramaic, "Rabboni!" (which means Teacher).

Jesus appears to Mary Magdalene

Theme Christ has risen from the dead and will wipe away all our tears.

Setting Outside the tomb of Jesus

Major Characters
- Mary Magdalene
- Jesus

Plot

Introduction and Rising Action

1. Mary Magdalene is weeping outside of Jesus's tomb.
2. Two angels ask Mary why she is weeping.
3. She is confused and afraid that someone has stolen Jesus's body.

Climax

4. When Mary turns around she sees another man. Assuming him to be a gardener, she asks him where Jesus's body has gone.
5. Jesus speaks her name, "Mary," and she recognizes him.

Falling Action and Resolution

6. He sends Mary to the disciples to tell them that he is risen from the dead.

Jesus Appears to the Disciples
Luke 24.36-49

Key Verse

Luke 24.44

Then he said to them, "These are my words that I spoke to you while I was still with you, that everything written about me in the Law of Moses and the Prophets and the Psalms must be fulfilled."

After his resurrection, Jesus appears to his disciples

Theme | Christ the risen Lord appears to his disciples, fulfilling all the Scriptures.

Setting | A house in Jerusalem

Major Characters |
- The disciples
- Jesus

Plot

Introduction and Rising Action

1. The disciples are together talking about Jesus being raised from the dead.
2. Suddenly, Jesus simply appears in their midst.
3. The disciples are scared and think they are seeing a ghost.

Climax

4. He calms the disciples by inviting them to touch his hands and feet. He also eats some fish for them see.
5. Jesus opens the disciples' minds to understand the Scriptures and to see that he is one who fulfills all the Law, the Prophets, and the Psalms (the whole Old Testament).
6. He commissions them as witnesses to proclaim Christ to all nations.

Falling Action and Resolution

7. Jesus promises to clothe them with power from on high.

Eastertide

. . . .

The Ascension of Christ

For forty days after his resurrection, Jesus revealed himself alive to his disciples.
On the fortieth day, he ascended to heaven to take his place
as Lord and Christ at God's right hand.
Ten days after this, on the fiftieth day after his resurrection,
he would send to us the promise of the Father –
the Holy Spirit, the pledge of our salvation.
Here we ponder the wonder of God's working,
from Easter Sunday to the Spirit's descent at Pentecost.

The Great Commission
Matthew 28.16-20

Key Verse

Matthew 28.18-20

And Jesus came and said to them, "All authority in heaven and on earth has been given to me. Go therefore and make disciples of all nations, baptizing them in the name of the Father and of the Son and of the Holy Spirit, teaching them to observe all that I have commanded you. And behold, I am with you always, to the end of the age."

"Go therefore, and make disciples of all nations . . ."

Theme | Christ the risen Lord sends his disciples to gather all nations into his Kingdom.

Setting | A mountain in Galilee

Major Characters

- Jesus
- The eleven disciples

Plot

Introduction and Rising Action

1. The disciples travel to a mountain in Galilee where Jesus has directed them.
2. When Jesus comes they worship him, but some doubt.

Climax

3. Jesus declares that all authority in heaven and on earth has been given to him.
4. He commissions his disciples to go and make disciples of all nations, baptizing them in the name of the Father and of the Son and of the Holy Spirit, and to teach them to observe all that he had commanded.

Falling Action and Resolution

5. Jesus promises that he is with them always, to the end of the age.

The Ascension of Christ
Acts 1.6-11

Key Verse

Acts 1.8

"But you will receive power when the Holy Spirit has come upon you, and you will be my witnesses in Jerusalem and in all Judea and Samaria, and to the end of the earth."

Theme

Christ ascends to the right hand of the Father where he reigns until all his enemies are put under his feet.

Setting

The Mount of Olives

Jesus ascends to the right hand of Father

Major Characters

- Jesus
- The disciples
- Two angelic men

Plot

Introduction and Rising Action

1. Jesus is talking with his disciples on the Mount of Olives. They ask him if it is time for him to restore the kingdom to Israel.

2. Jesus explains that only the Father knows the times for these things.

3. He promises to send the Holy Spirit to empower them to be his witnesses to the whole world.

Climax

4. As he is speaking he lifts off the ground and ascends into the sky until the clouds hide him.

5. The disciples are left staring into the sky.

Falling Action and Resolution

6. Two angelic men appear and ask the disciples what they are doing.

7. They tell them that Jesus has ascended to heaven and remind them that Jesus promised to return in the same way.

 Old Testament Foundation: The Triumph of the Son of Man (Daniel 7)

Elijah Taken into Heaven, 2 Kings 2

As Elijah was taken up into heaven never to taste death, so the risen Lord is taken up into heaven and eternal life.

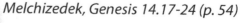

Melchizedek, Genesis 14.17-24 (p. 54)

The Lord Jesus ascends to the right hand of the Father where he waits for his enemies to be made a footstool for his feet, where he is both king and priest forever after the order of Melchizedek.

Pentecost

. . . .

The Coming of the Holy Spirit

*On Pentecost we commemorate the descent of the Holy Spirit to earth
on Christ's believers, his infilling of the people of God, the Church.
Through him, the third person of the Trinity,
Jesus our Lord is now present with his people.
The Spirit is the guarantee of the promised inheritance to come.
We ponder the fullness and mystery of our God's person and work
in our celebration on Trinity Sunday.*

The Coming of the Holy Spirit
Acts 2.1-47

Key Verse

Acts 2.2-4

And suddenly there came from heaven a sound like a mighty rushing wind, and it filled the entire house where they were sitting. And divided tongues as of fire appeared to them and rested on each one of them. And they were all filled with the Holy Spirit and began to speak in other tongues as the Spirit gave them utterance.

Theme

The Lord sends his Holy Spirit, personally dwelling among his people to empower and guide us.

Setting

A house in Jerusalem

Major Characters

•   Many followers of Jesus

•   A diverse international crowd of Jews

Plot

Introduction and Rising Action

1.   A large group of Jesus's followers are gathered in Jerusalem during the Jewish festival of Pentecost. Pentecost celebrated the firstfruits of the wheat harvest.

The Holy Spirit comes on the believers at Pentecost

Climax

2. Suddenly there is a sound like a mighty rushing wind.

3. The Holy Spirit descends in the form of "divided tongues as of fire" that enable the Apostles to proclaim the Gospel in several foreign languages.

4. People had come from all over the world for the festival. Each of them heard the Gospel in their own language.

5. Peter, the leader of the Apostles, stood up in the crowd and declared boldly that the arrival of the Holy Spirit marks the dawn of "the last days."

Falling Action and Resolution

6. According to Peter, the arrival of the Holy Spirit at Pentecost is the sign that "God has made him both Lord and Christ, this Jesus whom you crucified" (2.36).

7. After he preaches, the listeners are convicted to repent and receive baptism as a sign of their faith in Jesus as the Christ, sent from God.

8. The early Church shares everything in common, listening to the Apostles' teachings, and praising God.

Old Testament Foundation: Dry Bones Can Live Again (Ezekiel 37)

The Valley of Dry Bones, Ezekiel 37.1-14 (p. 112)

The Lord fulfills his vision to Ezekiel when he sends forth his Spirit and gives eternal life to his people.

The Spirit Spoke by the Prophets, Joel 2.28-32 (p. 126)

The Spirit of God that spoke by the prophets is poured out on the Church, signaling the inauguration of the last days.

85 | Paul's Missionary Journeys
Acts 22.1-21

Key Verse

Acts 22.7-9

"And I fell to the ground and heard a voice saying to me, 'Saul, Saul, why are you persecuting me?' And I answered, 'Who are you, Lord?' And he said to me, 'I am Jesus of Nazareth, whom you are persecuting.' Now those who were with me saw the light but did not understand the voice of the one who was speaking to me."

Paul shares the testimony of his conversion and calling

Theme   As ambassadors of the kingdom, the Church proclaims Jesus as Lord.

Setting   The Temple in Jerusalem

Major Characters
- Paul
- A crowd of Jews
- Roman soldiers

Plot

Introduction and Rising Action

1. Paul has been attacked by a crowd in the Temple in Jerusalem, and Roman soldiers have detained him for questioning.
2. He asks if he can address the crowd.
3. Paul tells the crowd that he also once hated and persecuted the followers of Jesus.

Climax

4. However, one day on the way to persecute believers in Damascus, the Lord appeared to him.
5. After three days of blindness, Paul was baptized by Ananias.
6. Paul then escaped from harm in Jerusalem, having been warned in a vision.

Falling Action and Resolution

7. The Lord sent Paul to the Gentiles to proclaim the Gospel.

Kingdomtide

. . . .

The Last Times: The Story Continues Today

*The Season after Pentecost, or Kingdomtide,
is a season of Christ's headship, harvest, and hope.
As Christus Victor, Jesus is exalted at God's right hand.
He is the head of the body, the Church, and he is Lord of the harvest,
empowering his people to bear witness of his saving grace in the world
and gather the harvest of souls so ripe for reaping.
Likewise, this is a season of the blessed hope, as we look to
Christ's sure return to complete God's salvation for the world.*

Paul, Ambassador in Chains
Acts 16.16-34

Key Verse

Acts 16.30-31

Then he brought them out and said, "Sirs, what must I do to be saved?" And they said, "Believe in the Lord Jesus, and you will be saved, you and your household."

Theme

As ambassadors of God's Kingdom, the Church suffers with Christ in order to be glorified with him.

Setting

Philippi

The Apostle Paul imprisoned for his Gospel ministry

Major Characters

- Paul
- Silas – Paul's traveling partner
- Lydia – a merchant
- Jailer

Plot

Introduction and Rising Action

1. Paul and Silas preach the Gospel in Philippi.
2. Lydia, a merchant, hears the message and believes. She is baptized along with her whole household.
3. While in Philippi, Paul and Silas are imprisoned for casting the demon out of a young girl.

Climax

4. In prison, Paul and Silas are singing and praising the Lord.
5. Suddenly, all the doors of the prison open and their chains fall off.
6. Paul stops the Jailer from killing himself, telling him that no one has escaped.
7. The jailer is amazed and asked how he can be saved. Paul tell him "Believe in the Lord Jesus, and you will be saved, you and your household."

Falling Action and Resolution

8. The jailer and his whole household believe and are baptized.
9. He brings Paul and Silas to his house for a joyful feast.

Old Testament Foundation: Daniel in the Lions' Den

Daniel in the Lions' Den, Daniel 6 (p. 116)

As the Lord delivered Daniel from the mouth of the lion, so the Lord delivered Paul from terrible opposition and threats as he preached the Gospel (2 Tim. 4.16-18).

Salvation to the World
Acts 10.34-43

Key Verse

Acts 10.42-43

And he commanded us to preach to the people and to testify that he is the one appointed by God to be judge of the living and the dead. To him all the prophets bear witness that everyone who believes in him receives forgiveness of sins through his name.

Theme

By his own grace, God has invited everyone everywhere into his Kingdom through faith in Jesus Christ.

Setting

The whole earth

Repentance and forgiveness of sins in the name of Jesus proclaimed to all nations

Major Characters

- The Holy Spirit
- The Apostles
- The Church

Plot

Introduction and Rising Action

1. The Apostles gave witness to Christ the risen Lord.
2. They proclaimed that in Jesus, God had made a way for men and women, boys and girls of every nation, culture, class, and station to have salvation and eternal life in his Kingdom.
3. They entrusted the Gospel to the Church as the words of eternal life.
4. Generations of Christians have proclaimed the Gospel of Christ in every nation.
5. One day the Lord will return and gather his people from the whole earth to be with him forever.

The Communion of Saints in Church History
Revelation 5

Key Verse

Revelation 5.9-10

And they sang a new song, saying, "Worthy are you to take the scroll and to open its seals, for you were slain, and by your blood you ransomed people for God from every tribe and language and people and nation, and you have made them a kingdom and priests to our God, and they shall reign on the earth."

Theme

The Church continues to expand God's Kingdom into every tribe and language and people and nation until he returns.

Setting

Multiple

Major Characters

- The Lord
- The Church
- The saints of the Lord

Christ is ransoming for God saints from every tribe and language and people and nation

Christian Martyrs (Rome, first to fourth centuries)

Sharing in his suffering and death (Philippians 3.10)

Early Christians faced persecution and death at the hands of the Roman Empire. Even being fed to lions could not stop the Church from proclaiming Christ!

Augustine of Hippo (North Africa, fourth to fifth century)

Transformed by the renewing of the mind (Romans 12.2)

Augustine fought for the truth of the Gospel in the face of many false teachers. The enemy has always tried to twist the Scriptures, but the Church has faithfully held to the teachings of the Apostles.

St. Francis of Assisi
(Italy, twelfth to thirteenth century)

Preach the Gospel to all creation (Mark 16.15)

St. Francis rejected a comfortable life and embraced suffering and difficulty for the sake of the Gospel. Men and women across history have accepted the calling of God to a life of prayer and prophetic witness to the world.

Martin Luther
(Germany, fifteenth to sixteenth century)

Not ashamed of the Gospel (Romans 1.16)

Martin Luther stood against Church leaders who abandoned the Gospel in favor of money and power. Reformers have always called the Church back to the Lord and back to her true identity.

Martin Luther King, Jr.
(United States of America, twentieth century)

Let justice roll down (Amos 5.24)

Martin Luther King, Jr. led oppressed and impoverished people in a fight for justice and equality. He was assassinated for his work. Across history, saints of the Lord have given their lives in pursuit of Christ and his Kingdom.

Mother Teresa of Calcutta
(India, twentieth century)

To the least of these (Matthew 25.40)

Mother Teresa founded a missionary society that ministers to the needs of some of the sickest, poorest, most broken people in the world. The Church has always sought to minister to the lowest and least in the world with the compassion and love of Jesus.

The Return of Christ
Revelation 19

Key Verse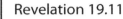

Revelation 19.11

Then I saw heaven opened, and behold, a white horse! The one sitting on it is called Faithful and True, and in righteousness he judges and makes war.

Theme 》

Christ is the savior who will destroy the devil and deliver humanity from sin and death forever.

Setting

John's vision of the final battle

Christ will come again and destroy death and the devil forever

Major Characters

- John – the one seeing the vision
- Jesus – a conquering warrior on a white horse
- The beast and the false prophet – enemies of God

Plot

Introduction and Rising Action

1. A great multitude of people praises the Lord for the vindication of the saints.
2. They cry out, "Hallelujah" for the great wedding supper of the Lamb has arrived, and his Bride is ready.

Climax

3. Jesus comes as a warrior on a white horse to do battle against evil. He is called Faithful and True, the Word of God, and King of kings and Lord of lords.
4. Under the leadership of the beast, the forces of wickedness draw up battle lines against the Lord, but an angel announces the destruction of the wicked before the battle even begins.

Falling Action and Resolution

5. Christ's victory is decisive and swift. He conquers God's enemies and throws them into the lake of fire.

 ### Old Testament Foundation: The Culmination and Fulfillment of the Promise

The Protoevangelium, Genesis 3.15 (p. 40)

With the Second Coming of Jesus Christ to restore all things under the rule of God, the original promise that was given in Genesis after the Fall, was fulfilled. God's promise to overcome evil and destroy the evil one comes to its completion in Christ's final victory.

The New Heaven and New Earth
Revelation 21.1-7, 22.1-5

Key Verse

Revelation 21.3-4

And I heard a loud voice from the throne saying, "Behold, the dwelling place of God is with man. He will dwell with them, and they will be his people, and God himself will be with them as their God. He will wipe away every tear from their eyes, and death shall be no more, neither shall there be mourning, nor crying, nor pain anymore, for the former things have passed away."

A new heaven and a new earth

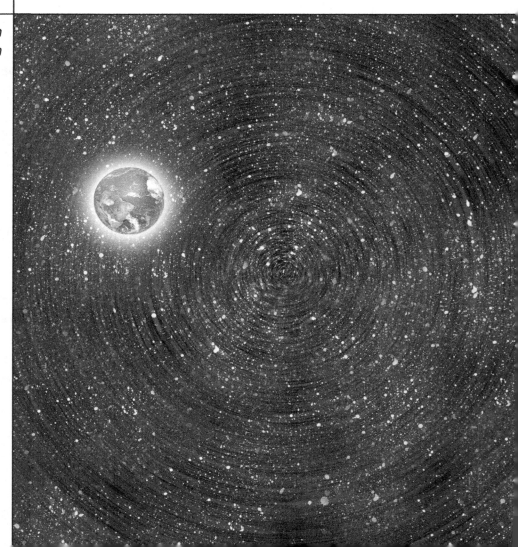

Theme God brings his kingdom blessing to all creation forever.

Setting John's vision of a new heaven and a new earth

Major Characters
- John – the one seeing the vision
- God on his throne
- John's angelic guide

Plot

Introduction and Rising Action

1. John sees a new heaven and a new earth.
2. The holy city, the New Jerusalem descend from the heaven to the earth.

Climax

3. The voice of God declares from the throne that his eternal dwelling place is among his people.
4. All signs of sin, the curse, evil, and death are wiped away. God is making all things new.
5. John sees a river of the water of life flowing from the throne of God and of the Lamb. The water feeds the tree of life that is for the healing of the nations.
6. The servants of God will live forever in his presence seeing him face to face. The Lord will be their light forever.

Falling Action and Resolution

7. The angel leaves John with the promise of the trustworthiness of his Word, and of the soon return of Christ.

. . . and the Story will never end . . .

Made in the USA
Middletown, DE
10 November 2022